Moments of Commitment:
Years of Growth

Moments of Commitment:

Years of Growth

Evangelism and Christian Education

by David L. Bartlett
and Ruth Fowler

CBP Press

St. Louis, Missouri

Library of Congress Cataloging-in-Publication Data

Bartlett, David Lyon, 1941-
    Moments of commitment.

    Includes index.
    1. Christian educations—Philosophy.   2. Evangelistic
work. I. Fowler, Ruth. I. Title.
BV1464.B378 1987   268   87-14096
ISBN 0-8272-0451-5

Printed in the United States of America

Contents

Contents

Dedication

This book and, more importantly, the evangelism and Christian education which will grow out of it, is respectfully dedicated to the memory of Donald A. Courtney (1929-1986). Donald Courtney dedicated his life's work to helping people in their journeys of faith through Christian education. He was tireless in his efforts to enable Christians both to reach outward to others to share the message of God's love and to reach inward to learn and grow in their personal spiritual journeys.

From 1966-1986, Courtney served as Executive Secretary for the Board of Christian Education, Church of God, Anderson, Indiana. During this time he touched many individual lives and the words of those friends and colleagues speak most eloquently about his life and work.

His influence lives on. The teaching ministries of the Church of God are deeper and richer today because of him. Many persons are actively participating and serving in the Church of God today because of Don. His involvement in ecumenical work extended the ministries of the Church of God into widening circles of influence. Not only is Don's leadership missed in the Church of God but in a variety of ways ecumenically and in the Anderson community. Don felt a oneness with God's people everywhere. —*Kenneth Prunty*

A mentor freely gives and shares with another person. A mentor helps that person develop faith in one's self and guides the development of potential that otherwise might have remained undeveloped. . . . The mentor has passed and the mantle has fallen. . . . We must pick up the mantle and continue the race. I do not feel qualified to carry the total mantle. . . . I invite you to carry with me the challenge for Christian education inspired by Don Courtney. —*Lynn Ridehour*

He was totally expendable for the cause of Christian education. His investment in equipping others to continue planning for the future will be his lasting, multiplying gift to the church. —*Betty Jo Hutchison*

Introduction

I was perplexed and reactive when I first heard a church growth advocate state, "One of the reasons mainline churches aren't growing is because Christian education materials do not call people to faith in Jesus Christ." I've since heard that statement expressed in a variety of ways and no longer become defensive about Christian education resources. Instead I have begun to explore the issue concerning the relationship between Christian education and evangelism. Do the curriculum resources presume that participants in the learning experience have made a commitment to follow Christ? Or is the possibility of such a commitment offered by the resources? Does the training of teachers of Christian education in the local church include the possibility that the spirit may present a moment or situation when the call to faith might be shared both in explicit and implicit ways? Do the Christian education committee and evangelism committee in the congregation take time to talk with each other and plan with each other?

In May of 1985, when the Education for Christian Life and Mission (ECLM) program committee was meeting, several denominations suggested an interest in exploring the intersection of Christian education with evangelism, church growth, and new church development. Donald A. Courtney, to whom this book is dedicated, was one of the persons who urged that ECLM initiate such a consultation. Subsequent to that meeting a design team of ECLM representatives was appointed and later joined to a similar design team from the Evangelism Working Group of the NCCC. This new team designed a consultation which was held at the Cabrini Center, October 20-22, 1986. The purpose of the Consultation was:

> to bring together persons on denominational staffs with evangelism/ church growth, Christian education, and new church development responsibilities to explore the issues and opportunities that exist among these ministry activities.

Participants to the consultation were sent background documents including a monograph, *Evangelism and Christian Education: Partners in Ministry,* by Garland Knott, Professor of Religion, Methodist College, Fayetteville, N.C. The principle speaker was Dr. David Bartlett, ABC pastor of Lake Shore Baptist Church, Oakland, California. His addresses are included in this book. The week of the consultation gave participants in education, evangelism, and church growth an opportunity not only to respond to Dr. Bartlett's presentations, but also to raise questions and explore issues with each other. An additional opportunity was offered to denominational representatives to caucus around concerns of Christian education and evangelism.

As a result of the consulation, partners to the dialogue gained greater clarity about possibilites for some merging of the interests and actions between Christian education and evangelism. At least two of the denominations there fostered a dialogue between Christian education and evangelism that has continued and that is now resulting in major program directions within the denomination. Further, because the participants perceived this issue to be important to the congregation, a suggestion was made that a study book for congregations be developed. A fervent hope and prayer is that Christians engaged in the vital ministry of the local church might continue to call people to faith, nurture them in that faith, and send them forth to serve Christ in the world. We believe that a partnership between Christian education and evangelism can be effectively used to this end.

Several persons deserve special recognition and thanks. Ima Jean Kidd, Director of Special Learning Needs, Leisure, and Outdoor Education for ECLM, has shepherded this book throughout the process of gathering materials, finding writers, and preparing it for publication. Rev. Ruth Fowler, Christian writer and educator, wrote the group session plans, leader's notes, and other planning materials for local congregations. Dr. David L. Bartlett provided the readings on which the study guide is based. Rev. Herbert H. Lambert, editor of CBP Press, book publisher of the Christian Church (Disciples of Christ), edited the book. And CBP Press published it. Dorothy R. Savage, Director of Educational Development for ECLM, reviewed the manuscript and made much-appreciated improvements.

—*Dr. Arthur O. Van Eck*, Executive Director, ECLM

Notes for the Leader

This study has been produced with three specific goals in mind:

—To provide the opportunity for church members to look at their personal faith journeys and their priorities for sharing their faith stories.

—To encourage church members to look at the ways in which evangelism and Christian education have been expressed in their denomination, their church, and their lives.

—To motivate church members creatively to combine Christian education and evangelism in their congregation and community.

Who?

This study is written for local church groups to be used by pastors, planners and congregation members. Some groups who might be interested in this study include faith sharing groups, planning councils and boards, membership development groups, and regular study groups such as Sunday school classes. In using this study, Christian education committees and evangelism committees would be stimulated and broadened in their work. Perhaps the church board would also be willing to enter this study.

One way to decide whom to invite to participate is first to thoroughly review this book. Next, think about your goals for the study. As leaders, what do you dream will happen as a result of this study? What hopes do you have? Which church members do you think would be most excited about working on a new relationship between evangelism and Christian education? Who works in Christian education in your congregation? In evangelism concerns?

The persons already most commited to these areas of work will be naturals for the study. But don't limit the study there! One goal of the study is to involve new people, to get more people energized about the possibilities of a partnership between evangelism and Christian education.

When?

Another part of deciding who will be invited to participate is deciding what kind of time commitment the group will be asked to make. One first step might be an informal survey of possible participants, asking them specifically what kind of commitment they are willing to make. Would they be willing to come for three sessions? for six? Would they prefer a one-day workshop? A weekend retreat? Also, how does this study "fit" with whatever else is going on? Timing is important.

What?

The study guide is written to provide the greatest possible flexibility in planning your study experience. The reading material is three lectures by David L. Bartlett. Following each reading there are two group sessions of one hour each. You may combine these to one session if your group is only meeting three times. The Alternative Plans section will give you specific suggestions for doing this. There are also suggestions for a weekend retreat or one-day workshop. You will know your group best. Read the activities and look at the plans, then decide what is best for your situation and people.

It may be that as your group ends the regularly scheduled sessions, some members will want to go further in their study and work. A section called Follow-up Possibilities is included for continued work by individuals or by the group.

Where?

The sessions include two forms of group work. Some of the sessions, including the closing worship, are for everyone to participate in at once. Your location will need to seat everyone comfortably, preferably in a circle so that participants can see one another easily. Some of the sessions include working in small groups or pairs. It will be helpful if the seats are movable so people can rearrange them when needed. If your group is small, consider having the meetings in a home or in a small room so the group does not feel lost in a large space. You will need space for wall posters, for newsprint, and for individuals to write.

How?

After the planning and first session of the study, you may want to share the leadership of the group with others. You might ask for volunteers to plan different sections of the study or you might ask for people to plan whole sessions. However the leadership is shared, it might be best for one person to gather all the materials needed in advance. Here is a list of what you will need for the study:

newsprint
felt-tip markers
coloring tools (crayons, colored felt-tip pens, etc.)
plain white paper (regular size)
masking tape
writing paper
pencils

Claiming Who We Are

Session at a Glance

Opening (5 minutes)—Get-Acquainted Activity
Story Lines (30 minutes)—Looking at the Ways Faith Grows
Spidergrams (20 minutes)—Sharing Our Own Stories
Closing Worship (5 minutes)—Celebration Prayer

Preparation

Because this is the first meeting, no one will have prepared outside work. In advance, call three people and ask them each to read and be prepared to summarize one of the faith stories presented in Reading #1 (St. Augustine, Dorothy Day, David Bartlett). Have photocopies of Reading #1 and of the Celebration Prayer (closing worship) available for each group member. Write the question for the opening on newsprint or chalkboard. The materials needed for this session are: newsprint, at least three markers, writing paper, pens.

If time allows, call each potential group member with a personal invitation to this first session. Pray for the group members individually and for their interaction with each other.

Opening—Get-Acquainted Activity

Write this question on newsprint or chalkboard where everyone can see it as they arrive: "How old were you when you first began to call yourself a Christian?" When the group has gathered ask persons to introduce themselves and to answer the question. For some the identity as "Christian" has always been part of their lives, for others there has been a definite time of conversion, and for still others a confirmation or specific event(s) will be most significant.

Story Lines—Looking at the Way Faith Grows

1. Divide into three small groups of at least two persons each. Each group will study a different faith story. Ask the persons who prepared in advance to tell the group their summary of the faith story they were given.

2. Give each group newsprint and a marker. Ask the participants to draw a timeline or story line which marks the most significant events in the lives of each of the three persons studied. As they work on the story lines, encourage members to include not only dates and events, but the feelings expressed by the people.

3. After twenty minutes ask the small groups to come back together and spend the next ten minutes sharing the story lines they created.

Spidergrams—Sharing Our Own Stories

1. Ask group members to work individually in this activity. Give them writing paper and pens. Ask them to write one word in the middle of the page telling how they *feel* about their faith journey right now. Then, using that word as a focus point, write as many different words, names, dates, or ideas as they can think of on the paper. The idea is to work quickly, using the first thoughts that come to them. After five minutes, move on in the activity.

2. Now ask participants to draw a circle around their first feeling word. Drawing spider legs, connect different words that go together for them. (Show illustration No. 1.1, on p. 00 if needed.) After five minutes move on in the activity.

3. Come back together as a large group and share some of the feeling words and the spider leg connections that make up participants' faith stories.

Illustration 1.1

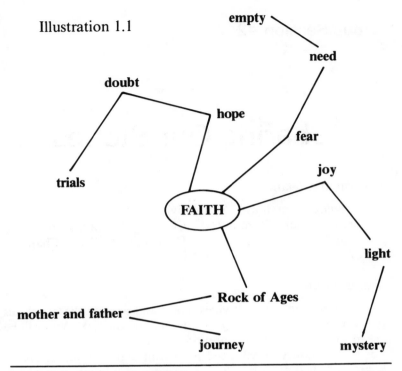

Closing—Celebration Prayer

Read the following prayer responsively, with participants inserting their individual petitions:

Leader: Creator God, we praise your holy name.
People: And we celebrate the wisdom with which you planned and made our world.
Leader: We are especially grateful for the gift of the Savior in our lives
People: And we celebrate the gift we are to one another in the journey of faith we take together.
Leader: We ask for the presence of the Holy Spirit with this group as we study together and live and work in this community.
People: And we celebrate your presence with _____ [group may add names of persons they wish to pray for].
All: These things we pray in the name of the Creator, the Savior, and the Holy Spirit. Amen.

Sharing Our Stories

Session at a Glance

> *Opening* (5 minutes)—Story Giving
> *Brainstorming* (30 minutes)—Claiming the Bible's Stories
> *Four Questions* (20 minutes)—Discovering the Main Character
> *Closing* (5 minutes)—Story Giving

Preparation

Read through the activities again and answer the questions for yourself. Do the Four Questions activity on p. 00. You will be asked to share the story you write in the opening of the session. For this session you will need newsprint and markers or chalkboard and chalk for a brainstorming session and writing materials and pens for the Four Questions activity. Pray for group members and for the work you will be doing together. Have photocopies of Reading #2 ready to hand out at the close of the session.

Opening—Story Giving

Ask members to share any thoughts or feelings they have had since last session. Tell the group that you also have done the activity that is planned for them in this session and ask them to receive from you the story you wrote. Share your story.

Brainstorming—Claiming the Bible's Stories

1. Introduce this activity by pointing out that the Bible is the richest source of stories in the Christian tradition and that both Christian education and evangelism activities depend upon the Bible as a sourcebook and foundation. Ask the participants to

take a few moments to think about what Bible stories they connect with Christian education or discipleship training and what Bible stories they connect to evangelism. Write their responses on newsprint or chalkboard where all can see it. Remind the group that brainstorming is "thinking aloud together" and encourage participants to share all their thoughts.

2. Put stars by the stories that are on both lists, if any, to point to the common stories. Take the next fifteen minutes to talk about the stories. Some questions for discussion starters might include:

What do you feel when you hear the stories?

What do the main characters do to bring about the events in the story?

How are you alike or different from the main characters?

Are you more familiar with the stories about discipleship or evangelism?

What relationship do you see in the two sets of stories?

Are any decisions called for?

3. Ask the group to think about the three life stories shared in Reading #1. Ask the group to imagine what stories these three persons would put on the lists and why.

Four Questions—Discovering the Main Character

1. Give writing paper and pens to participants. Ask them to think of themselves as the main character in a story—their story. In order to write the story they need to know more about this main character. Have them learn about themselves by writing a one- or two-word answer to each of the following questions:

If I were to describe in one word the strength of my life, it would be _____ .

If I were to describe in one word a need in my life, it would be _____ .

The song title or book title that best describes my life at the present moment is ――――――――――――――――――――― .

I feel best when ――――――――――――――――――――――――― .

2. Ask the group members to look at their answers and then to write a short story imagining what their main character (themselves) would do if asked to tell the story of Jesus to a child. Give them ten minutes to write.

3. After the group members have finished writing their stories ask them to look at the stories and decide if their stories would be best used in Christian education or evangelism. Talk about their answers. Point out that for many people the story of Jesus, as they have experienced it, is both a call to discipleship and an evangelical message. It is the beginning point of both endeavors—people experiencing Christ and telling others what Christ has meant in their lives.

Closing—Story Giving

Spend the last five minutes sharing the stories participants wrote. Perhaps placing the stories in the center of the group and joining hands. Sharing is voluntary. Some people may also want to share the answers to their questions. Give thanks for the witness and nurturing that has happened and that can happen through sharing of stories.

After the Meeting

Hand out copies of Reading #2 for participants to read before next week. Tell them that you will be concentrating on the first part of the reading in session four and the second part of the reading in session five.

Group Session #3

Education-Evangelism Choice

Session at a Glance

Opening (5 minutes)—Putting Us in the Picture
Conversion or Nurture (30 minutes)—A Continuing Debate
Family of Faith Crest (20 minutes)—Showing Our Colors
Closing (5 minutes)—Changing History

Preparation

If possible gather information about your denomination's history to share with the group in the opening segment. Where and when did mission work develop? Where and when did Christian education begin? Are there assumptions about which is most important? If the information about the denomination is unavailable, then ask the same questions about your congregation. You may want to read Garland Knott's work in the Additional Reading section. Gather the materials you will need for this session: newsprint and markers, plain white paper and coloring tools.

Opening—Putting Us in the Picture

Begin by sharing what you learned about your denomination's history. If you do not have this information ask the group. Perhaps someone in the group knows, or would like to find out. Point out that the study today centers on Paul and the earliest Christians, and we who are connected to these Christians through our continuing common history. Emphasize that there was then, and continues to be, a tension between evangelism and education.

19

Conversion or Nurture—A Continuing Debate

1. Ask the group to divide into pairs. Ask one person in each pair to choose to be the "conversion" priority (Paul's perspective in the reading) and the other to choose to be the education or "nurture" priority (the perspective of the pastoral writings). They are to spend ten minutes (five minutes each) talking with each other about why their priority is important.

2. Come back into the large group, and ask the groups to report on some of the impressions the debate made on them. Ask them what the difference between the two priorities is today, for them, as compared with Paul and the early Christians. Spend about fifteen minutes in this discussion.

3. Ask the group members to think of one or two words or phrases to describe the reason they believe Christian education (nurture) is an important priority and one or two words or phrases to describe the reason they believe evangelism (conversion) is an important priority. They will want to remember these words to help in the next activity.

Family of Faith Crest—Showing Our Colors

1. Pass out plain white paper and coloring tools. Ask participants to design family crests in the shape of a shield or any other shape they wish. Divide the crests into four parts. On the left side put two parts—the early church view of nurturing and the early church view of conversion. On the right side put two parts—your own view of nurturing and your own view of conversion. The crests may use either words, names of influential educators and evangelists, or drawings to represent the four different ideas. (Show Illustration 3.1 if needed.) Allow participants to work for about 10 minutes.

2. Come together as a group and share the Family of Faith Crests that the participants have made.

Closing—Changing History

Introduce the closing with these thoughts: Christians in the time of the New Testament knew that what they did would shape the future of Christianity. We don't think about ourselves as people who can change the course of history but we do. We stand as a gate between all those who have gone before and those who will come after us. We can use the gate as an entry to the Christian life or as a barrier. Let's spend a moment of silence considering where and how we want to change the patterns in our lives and in the life of our church.

Illustration 3.1

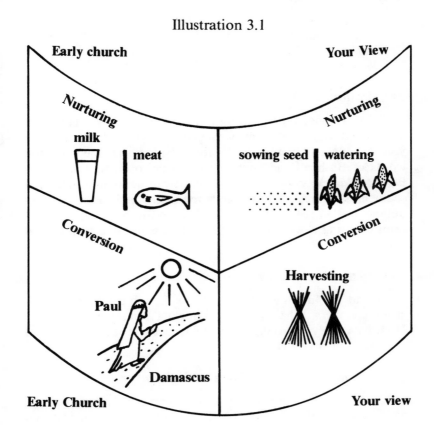

21

Evangelism-Education Circle

Session at a Glance

> *Opening* (5 minutes)—Catching Up
> *Bushnell and Edwards* (30 minutes)—Lives to Remember
> *Graffiti Wall* (20 minutes)—Words to Remember
> *Closing* (5 minutes)—Handwriting on the Wall

Preparation

Look over again the second part of Reading #2. Highlight quotes and ideas that seem particularly striking or important to you. Ask a group member to be able to summarize the work and words of Bushnell and another to be able to do the same with Edwards. Make copies of the quotes from denominational and ecumenical sources that are gathered at the end of this session outline. Gather the materials you will need for this session: newsprint covering a wall (tape in place before meeting begins) and markers.

Opening—Catching Up

Spend the first few minutes of this session catching up with group members. What have they thought about since last session? How have they noticed the interplay between conversion and nurture in their church?

Bushnell and Edwards—Lives to Remember

1. Ask group members who volunteered to summarize the work and words of each of these men. Have other group

members add any thoughts or ideas they might have about these two men. Spend about ten minutes in this activity.

2. Ask group members to tell about other people, from your denomination or congregation especially, who have made strong stands for an emphasis on evangelism or church education. These might include pastors of the church, missionaries or denominational workers, writers of church materials, etc. Spend another ten minutes in this activity.

3. Ask the group to think about evangelism and Christian education as two parts of a continuing circle. How might they be related to each other? What are other elements of the circle?

Graffiti Wall—Words to Remember

Pass out copies of the quotes. Ask the group to divide into pairs. Working together, from Reading #2 find quotes which are important to them. Ask them to write their quotes on the Graffiti Wall placing their initials after the quotes so the group will know who chose each. Spend about twenty minutes on the Graffiti Wall.

Closing—Handwriting on the Wall

Use Graffiti Wall as a litany. Divide group and alternate the readings. Or, ask persons to read the statements they identified after which all would respond, "This we believe."

After the Meeting

Hand out copies of Reading #3 and ask participants to be thinking about which of the churches described in the reading sounds most like their own church. Recruit volunteers to be able to summarize the work of each of the three churches for the group.

Possible Quotes for Graffiti Wall

The 1976 Policy Statement on Evangelism by the National Council of Churches Governing Board states:

> The commitment to Jesus Christ is a profound event. It is a *personal* event; by the power of the Holy Spirit sinners experience divine forgiveness and commit themselves to live obediently to Christ the living Lord. It is a *social* event; relationships with friends, neighbors and family are radically altered by the revolutionary demands and allowances of divine love. It is a *community* event; it engrafts one into the new community of believers, the church. It is a *public* event; new confrontations with the institutions of society occur. . . . The task of evangelism today is calling people to repentance, to faith in Jesus Christ, to study God's word, to continue steadfast in prayer, and to bearing witness to Him.

The Cooperative Curriculum Project of 1965, a Christian education planning group sponsored by the National Council of Churches and 16 participating denominations, stated the objective of the curriculum:

> The objective of Christian education is that all persons be aware of God, through God's self-disclosure, especially God's redeeming love as revealed in Jesus Christ, and that they respond in faith and love—to the end that they may know who they are and what their human situation means, grow as sons and daughters of God rooted in the Christian community, live in the Spirit of God in every relationship, fulfill their common discipleship in the world, and abide in the Christian hope.

The Mission and Evangelism statement approved by the Central Committee of the World Council of Churches in July, 1982, stated:

> Conversion happens in the midst of our historical reality and incorporates the totality of our life, because God's love is concerned with that totality. Jesus' call is an invitation to follow him joyfully, to participate in his servant body, to share with him in the struggle to overcome sin, poverty and death. . . . There is no evangelism without

solidarity; there is no Christian solidarity that does not involve sharing the knowledge of the kingdom which is God's promise to the poor of the earth.

The Vatican II documents included statements on both evangelism and Christian education:

On Christian education—
Since every Christian has become a new creature by rebirth from water and the Holy Spirit, so that [s]he may be called what [s]he truly is, a child of God, [s]he is entitled to a Christian education. Such an education does not merely strive to foster in the human person the maturity already described. Rather, its principal aims are these: that as the baptized person is gradually introduced into a knowledge of the mystery of salvation, [s]he may daily grow more conscious of the gift of faith which [s]he has received; that [s]he may learn to adore God the Father in spirit and in truth, especially through liturgical worship; that [s]he may be trained to conduct [her] his personal life in righteousness and in sanctity of truth, according to [her] his new standard of [woman]manhood. Thus, indeed, [s]he may grow into [woman]manhood according to the mature measure of Christ.

On evangelism—
Whenever God opens a door of speech for proclaiming the mystery of Christ, there should be announced to all [women] men with confidence and constancy the living God, and He whom He has sent for the salvation of all, Jesus Christ. Thus when the Holy Spirit opens their heart non-Christians may beleve and be freely converted to the Lord, and may sincerely cling to Him who, as "the way, the truth and the life," fulfills all their spiritual expectations, and even infinitely surpasses them. This conversion, to be sure, must be regarded as a beginning. Yet it is sufficient that a [woman] man realize that [s]he had been snatched away from sin and led into the mystery of the love of God, who has called [her] him to enter into a personal relationship with Him in Christ. For, by the workings of divine grace, the convert sets out on a spiritual journey.

Group Session #5

Finding Our Style

Session at a Glance

Opening (5 minutes)—Gift Discovery
How Some Churches Do It (30 minutes)—Looking at Options
Where Am I? (20 minutes)—Discovering My style
Closing (5 minutes)—Gift Giving

Preparation

Remind volunteers of their assignments before the meeting. Pray for your church and members of the group. Leaders may wish to record the information in *Where Am I—Discovering My Style*. Gather the materials needed for this session: masking tape, newsprint and markers, plain white paper, and pens for writing.

Opening—Gift Discovery

Ask group members as they arrive to take pieces of paper and write on them gifts or abilities they have that their church uses or could use. Ask them to write large and to sign their names. Emphasize that the gifts or abilities may take many different forms. Have them fold the papers and keep them until later in the group meeting.

How Some Churches Do It—Looking at Options

1. Ask the three volunteers to give brief summaries (about five minutes each) of the churches in Reading #3. Ask participants to listen for ways their church is like each church and ways their church is different from each church.

2. Spend the last fifteen minutes making lists of "Things We Give Thanks For" and "Ideas for Change" growing out of the study of the three churches. Encourage participants to be honest

about what they are thinking and to ask questions about one another's thoughts and ideas.

Where Am I?—Discovering My Style

1. Use masking tape to draw a line diagonally across the room. Tell participants the line represents a continuum from one extreme—emphasis on evangelism with little or no Christian education—to another extreme—emphasis on Christian education with no evangelism. Ask them to think about what mix of evangelism and Christian education they would like to find in their church. Which is prominent in the congregation—an emphasis on Christian education or evangelism? Ask them to go and stand on the place which identifies their perception of where their church is. Next ask them to identify where whey would like the church to be and go and stand on that spot. Many may choose approximately the same spot. That's okay. (See Illustration 5.1 for examples of spots on the line.)

2. Now ask them to remember the gifts or abilities they wrote on their papers and decide where on the continuum those gifts could be used. Ask them to move to those spots and open their papers where everyone can read the gifts they wrote.

3. Ask group members to say what their gifts are and why they chose those spots.

Closing—Gift-Giving

Point out that the line on which they stand is a part of their church, and ask persons to tape the papers on which they have written their gifts onto the spots in the line. Then ask them to move away from the line and look at their gifts. Pray a prayer of thanksgiving for the many gifts we bring to the community of faith.

Illustration 5.1

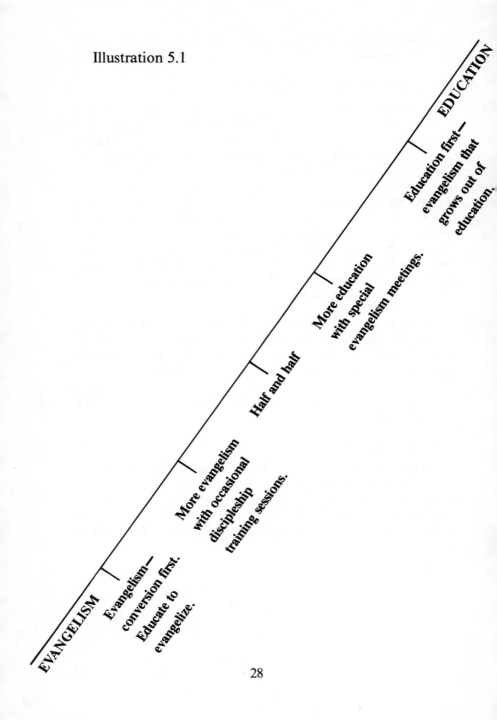

EDUCATION

Education first—
evangelism that
grows out of
education.

More education
with special
evangelism meetings.

Half and half

More evangelism
with occasional
discipleship
training sessions.

Evangelism—
conversion first.
Educate to
evangelize.

EVANGELISM

Celebrating Discipleship

Session at a Glance

Opening (5 minutes)—Sharing Thoughts
Discussion (30 minutes)—What Are the Possibilities?
Choosing a Course (20 minutes)—New Commitments
Closing (5 minutes)—Prayer for Discipleship

Preparation

Because this is the last session, you will want to be sure members have a chance to talk about their experiences in the group. If you wish to evaluate, there is an evaluation form at the end of this session, p. 00, that you may have them fill in and return after the meeting. Have photocopies of one form for each person. Review the last part of Reading #3 and the section titled Choosing a Course. Write the three statements from Bartlett's work below on newsprint or on a chalkboard where everyone can see it. Pray for the group. Gather the materials you will need: newsprint and markers, writing paper, and pens.

"Christian education which nurtures discipleship will not only deepen understanding, it will ask for commitment."

"Evangelism which calls for discipleship will not only seek commitment, it will encourage growth in understanding, and a deepening of the Christian gifts of faith, hope and love."

"The disciple (the converted and being-educated Christian) lives not for the sake of the self, nor for the sake of the church, but for the sake of Christ in the world."

Opening—Sharing Thoughts

Ask group members each to share one thought they have had during the last week about their church as related to evangelism and Christian education.

Discussion—What Are the Possibilities?

1. Ask the group members to read the three statements. What thoughts or ideas do the statements bring to mind? Spend about ten minutes in this sharing.

2. Divide into pairs and ask the pairs to share with one another about a time when they felt commitment and understanding grew in their life. Spend about ten minutes in this sharing.

3. Return to a large group and ask members to discuss how commitment and understanding can be encouraged in their lives, especially in their current church setting. Write ideas on the newsprint.

Choosing a Course—New Commitments

1. Review briefly for the group the section of Follow-up Possibilities. Ask group members to consider what kind of commitment they can make to helping their congregation in the tasks of evangelism and church education. Point out that we are all disciples by the definition in the first activity.

2. Ask members to turn with their backs to one another so they can pray and think without distractions. Tell them they are to consider making one new commitment to being a disciple. Ask them to write it down and keep it. Emphasize that the commitment is between them and God and will not be shared with the large group. Allow about ten minutes for this part of the activity.

3. Return to the large group. Spend the last five minutes of this activity sharing feelings. Ask members what they felt and thought when they were asked to make a commitment.

Closing—Prayer for Discipleship

Ask the group to compose together a prayer asking for a new commitment to discipleship, then read the prayer aloud. Work on newsprint to write the prayer. Ask each member to make a copy. During the coming week they are to mail the copy to the sharing partner during this session thanking them for participating.

After the Meeting

Ask those who are willing to fill in evaluation forms.

Evaluation Form

With 0 being the lowest rating and 5 being the highest, rate the following:

Circle One	Please Evalute:
0 1 2 3 4 5	Length of readings
0 1 2 3 4 5	Vocabulary of readings
0 1 2 3 4 5	Appropriateness of topics of readings
0 1 2 3 4 5	Choice of illustrations and stories in readings
0 1 2 3 4 5	Suitability of readings for group work
0 1 2 3 4 5	Kind of activities
0 1 2 3 4 5	Format of sessions
0 1 2 3 4 5	Amount of prayer and worship
0 1 2 3 4 5	Amount of work done in small groups
0 1 2 3 4 5	Amount of discussion activities
0 1 2 3 4 5	Leadership

Other comments: _____

_____

_____

Name (optional): _____

Follow-Up Possibilities

Here are some brief ideas for more involvement:

Group Activities

1. *Plan a Churchwide Focus*—Plan a one-evening session to pull together the best of what you did and learned. Perhaps an evening worship time could be available. Choose activities that involve other church members in ways that you enjoyed being involved.

2. *Make Recommendation*—If appropriate, make recommendations to the Christian education committee, the evangelism committee and/or the church board. What needs to be affirmed? What needs to be changed?

3. *Plan a Creative Worship*—One possibility is to plan a special worship service using stories, art, music, dance or whatever creative expressions you wish to tell the story of faith as you experience it.

4. *Learn from Other People*—Invite church leaders from different faith and ethnic groups to teach you about evangelism and Christian education. This could be a churchwide activity or an activity for your group's continued study.

5. *Plan a New Study*—Choose from the bibliography or from your denomination's resources, and continue your study together. One example would be studying the book *Storyweaving*, by Peter Morgan.

Individual Activities

1. *Tell Your Story*—Share your faith story (see session 1) with your family, and invite them to share theirs. You might also want to share your story with your Sunday school class or other group.

2. *Develop Your Gifts*—Remember your gifts (see session 5), and plan one way to develop a gift and use it in your church.

3. *Read More About It*—Pick an area that interests you and read more. For example are you interested in biography or in Bible study?

Sermon Ideas

1. *Augustine, Dorothy Day, and You*—Compare these three faith stories and talk about the ways you believe evangelism and Christian education are important to these three lives.

2. *Paul or the Pastorals*—Consider preaching on the ways you agree or disagree with Bartlett's juxtaposition of Paul and the pastorals.

3. *What Are We Supposed to Do?*—Look at the expectations of your church tradition and of your particular congregation in light of this study.

Alternative Plans

Perhaps your group would rather meet for a weekend retreat, a one-day workshop, or in three sessions. This section provides plans for those meetings. The activities are chosen from those given for the six-session plan.

Weekend Retreat

Plan your retreat for a place where participants can be out-of-doors part of the time, if at all possible. Most churches will want to finish in time for participants to attend services Sunday morning. This means beginning Friday evening and finishing Saturday evening in most cases. If your retreat place is close to the church you may want to continue through an early morning prayer time Sunday and then go to services together. Some congregations are having "stay at home" retreats.

Because a retreat must be planned in advance, you will want to enlist the volunteers needed for activities *before the retreat*. This will mean that participants can spend time together instead of preparing for the next session. If at all possible, have a book for each group member. If not, pass out photocopies of all three readings in advance of the retreat.

The time for the first session opening and closing and for the final closing have been lengthened to give more time for sharing.

Weekend at a Glance

Friday Evening

6:00 p.m. Dinner Together
7:30 p.m. Session 1 (1 1/2 hours):
   Opening (10 minutes)—Getting Acquainted
   Story Lines (30 minutes)—Looking at the Ways Faith Grows

Spidergrams (20 minutes)—Sharing Our Own Stories
Closing Worship (15 minutes)—Celebration Prayers
9:00 p.m. Fellowship Together

Saturday Morning

7:00 a.m. Breakfast Together
8:30 a.m. Session 2 (1 hour):
    Opening (5 minutes)—Story Giving
    Brainstorming (30 minutes)—Claiming the Bible's Stories
    Four Questions (20 minutes)—Discovering the Main Character
    Closing (5 minutes)—Story Giving
10:00 a.m. Coffee Break

10:30 a.m. Session 3 (1 hour):
    Opening (5 minutes)—Putting Us in the Picture
    Conversion or Nurture (30 minutes)—A Continuing Debate
    Family of Faith Crest (20 minutes)—Showing Our Colors
    Closing (5 minutes)—Changing History
12:00 Noon Lunch Together

Saturday Afternoon

1:00 p.m. Time Alone, with Friends, or with Nature
2:30 p.m. Session 4 (1 hour):
    Opening (5 minutes)—Catching Up
    Bushnell and Edwards (30 minutes)—Lives to Remember
    Graffiti Wall (20 minutes)—Words to Remember
    Closing (5 minutes)—Handwriting on the Wall
3:30 p.m. Coffee Break

4:00 p.m. Session 5 (1 hour):
    Opening (5 minutes)—Gift Discovery
    How Some Churches Do It (30 minutes)—Looking at Options
    Where Am I? (20 Minutes)—Discovering My Style
    Closing (5 minutes)—Gift Giving
6:00 p.m. Dinner Together

Saturday Evening

7:00 p.m. Session 6 (1 1/2 hours):
    Opening (5 minutes)—Sharing Thoughts
    Discussion (30 minutes)—What Are the Possibilities?

Choosing a Course (20 minutes)—New Commitments
Closing (20 minutes)—Prayer for Discipleship

One-Day Workshop

The one-day workshop plan is intense, with lots of work crowded into a short period of time. There is one opening, instead of one for each session, and there is one closing. The activities are the same as in the regular sessions, but the times have changed. There are two kinds of breaks suggested—coffee breaks and stretch breaks.

8:30—9:00 a.m. Get-Acquainted (Session 1 Opening)

9:00—9:45 a.m. Session One
  Story Lines (25 minutes)—Looking at the Ways Faith Grows
  Spidergrams (20 minutes)—Sharing Our Own Stories

9:45—10:00 a.m. Coffee Break

10:00—10:45 a.m. Session Two
  Brainstorming (25 minutes)—Claiming the Bible's Stories
  Four Questions (20 minutes)—Discovering the Main Character

10:45—11:00 a.m. Stretch Break

11:00—11:45 a.m. Session Three
  Conversion or Nurture (25 minutes)—A Continuing Debate
  Family of Faith Crest (20 minutes)—Showing Our Colors

12:00—1:00 p.m. Lunch Together

1:00—1:45 p.m. Session Four
  Bushnell and Edwards (25 minutes)—Lives to Remember
  Graffiti Wall (20 minutes)—Words to Remember

1:45—2:15 Stretch Break

2:15—3:00 p.m. Session Five
  How Some Churches Do It (25 minutes)—Looking at Options
  Where Am I? (20 Minutes)—Discovering My Style

3:00—3:15 p.m. Coffee Break

3:15—4:00 p.m. Session Six
Discussion (25 minutes)—What Are The Possibilities?
Choosing a Course (20 minutes)—New Commitments

4:00—4:15 p.m. Closing—Prayer for Discipleship (Session Six Closing)

Three-Session Plan

For some groups a commitment to six sessions is too much to ask. The following guide combines the six session plan into three sessions. Of course some of the activities have had to be eliminated. Others have been shortened. If, in studying the full six sessions you wish to choose different activities or lengths, please do so. You know your group best.

Session 1

Opening (5 minutes)—Getting Acquainted
Story Lines (20 minutes)—Looking at the Ways Faith Grows
Brainstorming (15 minutes)—Claiming the Bible's Stories
Spidergrams (15 minutes)—Sharing Our Own Stories
Closing Worship (5 minutes)—Celebration Prayers

Session 2

Opening (5 minutes)—Putting Us in the Picture
Conversion or Nurture (20 minutes)—A Continuing Debate
Bushnell and Edwards (15 minutes)—Lives to Remember
Family of Faith Crest (15 minutes)—Showing Our Colors
Closing (5 minutes)—Changing History

Session 3

Opening (5 minutes)—Gift Discovery
How Some Churches Do It (20 minutes)—Looking at Options
Discussion (15 minutes)—What Are the Possibilities?
Choosing a Course (15 minutes)—New Commitments
Closing (5 minutes)—Prayer for Discipleship

Reading #1

Faith Journeys

by David L. Bartlett

I begin with a guess, or more formally, a hypothesis. The faith journey of every committed Christian has included both the gift of evangelism and the gift of Christian education. Put more broadly, each of us lives out of both nurture and decision. Each of us lives out of moments of commitment and years of growth.

I choose three figures to see how nurture and commitment, conversion and growth, came together in their lives. Two of the cases are classic—the story of St. Augustine of Hippo and the story of Dorothy Day of the Catholic Worker Movement. The third case, because sharing is essential to understanding, is myself.

I will suggest for simplicity's sake that for Augustine a long process of nurture led to the classic moment of conversion. For Dorothy Day the decision to become a Christian and to be baptized was the beginning of a nurturing process that continued until the day she died. For myself it was some of the one and some of the other.

I

St. Augustine is second only to St. Paul as the model of Christian conversion. Unfortunately we know very little about any internal pressures or subtle nurturing that led Paul to his conversion, and we know very little of what moved him from new convert to apostle and theologian. Augustine, in his *Confessions* has given us much more.

The classic moment came in the garden at Milan. Augustine was in his early thirties. His journey to that place and that moment had included a vivid conviction of his own sinfulness.

39

Looking back later, he could see selfishness from the time he nursed at his mother's breast, and transgression in the famous incident with the pear tree. But more lively and painful was the young adult's guilt at his concupiscence. Augustine felt himself overcome by lust, though it needs to be noted that for most of the years of his life that lust had been expressed in a monogamous relationship with his concubine, with whom he had one son, and with whom he lived in an apparently loving relationship on terms which were neither unusual nor disgraceful in the Empire of that time.

Nonetheless, burdened by his sense of sin, Augustine says: "But I, a most wretched youth, most wretched from the very start of my youth, had even sought chastity of you, and had said, 'Give me chastity and continence, but not yet!'"[1]

Now a friend, Ponticianus, has come to visit. He relates to Augustine the virtues and faithfulness of certain Egyptian monks. Augustine turns to his friend, Alypius, greatly perturbed, crying: "What is the trouble with us? What is this? What did you hear?"[2] Then Augustine falls to weeping and moves off from Alypius to have some privacy. Augustine tells the rest of the story: "I flung myself down, how I do not know, under a certain fig tree, and gave free rein to my tears. The floods burst from my eyes, an acceptable sacrifice to you. . . . I spoke many things to you: 'And you, 0 Lord, how long? How long, 0 Lord, will you be angry forever? Remember not our past iniquities . . . . How long, how long? Tomorrow and tomorrow? Why not now? Why not in this very hour an end to my uncleanness?'"

"Such words I spoke, and with most bitter contrition I wept within my heart. And lo, I heard from a nearby house, a voice like that of a boy or girl, I know not which, chanting and repeating over and over, 'Take up and read. Take up and read!' Instantly, with altered countenance, I began to think most intently whether children made use of any such chant in some kind of game, but I could not recall hearing it anywhere."

So Augustine returns to Alypius, where he had left a volume of Paul's letters. "I snatched it up, opened it, and read in silence the chapter on which my eyes first fell: 'Not in rioting and drunkenness, not in chambering and impurities, not in strife and envying; but put you on the Lord Jesus Christ and make not provision for the flesh and its concupiscences.'"

Then Augustine concludes: "No further wished I to read, nor was there need to do so. Instantly, in truth, at the end of this sentence, as if before a peaceful light streaming into my heart, all the dark of doubt fled away."[3]

Shortly thereafter Augustine was baptized by St. Ambrose. Peter Brown describes the event: "Passing behind curtains, Augustine would descend, alone, stark naked, into a deep pool of water. Three times, Ambrose would hold his shoulders beneath the gushing fountain. Later, dressed in a pure white robe, [Augustine] would enter the main basilica ablaze with candles, and, amid the acclamations of the congregation, he and his fellow neophytes would take their place . . . by the altar, for a first participation in the mysteries of the Risen Christ."[4]

Here is a paradigmatic instance of sorrow for sin, a miraculous sign, conviction and conversion by the word of God, and a life changed radically, the change signed by baptism. All of that is true enough, but perhaps not quite true *enough*.

What the standard retellings of the story leave out is illustrated by the fact that at the time of his conversion Augustine was, for a second time, a catechumen of the church. Like many others of his time he had not been willing to make the final decision for baptism. Perhaps he held off for some time in part because he knew that if he were baptized he would have to give up the concubine whom he no doubt loved. As it happened, his concubine had some time since been forced to depart from him so that he could make a respectable marriage, and one wonders whether the loss of that human love made him at last more open to the love of God.

The fact that at the time of his conversion Augustine was already a catechumen is a sign of the fact that a remarkable history of nurturing, nudging, praying, and seeking led to his conversion.

"While I was still a boy," he writes, "I had heard of that eternal life promised to us through the humility of the Lord our God, who lowered himself to our pride. I was signed with the sign of his cross, and seasoned with his salt, as soon as I issued from my mother's womb."[5] The sign and the salt were marks of the catechumen.

The fact that Augustine says his faith began from the womb of his mother is deeply significant, for it is clear that next to God,

Augustine's greatest love was his mother, and her greatest goal was that her son should be baptized.

A woman of apparently great energy, vigor, faith, and persistence, Monica cajoled, besought, and especially prayed Augustine toward faith. When Augustine strayed off after the Manicheans, Monica first barred him from her house and then steadfastly prayed him toward the Catholic faith. "You put forth your hand from on high," says Augustine to the Almighty, "and you drew my soul out of that pit of darkness, when before you, my mother, your faithful servant, wept more for me than mothers weep for their children's dead bodies. By that spirit of faith which she had from you, she saw my death, and you graciously heard her, O Lord. Graciously you heard her, and you did not despise her tears when they flowed down from her eyes and watered the earth beneath, in whatever place she prayed."[6] In answer to this prayer, God sent Monica a vision of Augustine joined to her in faith. That vision kept her steadfast and confident as he wandered to and fro for nine years more.

Immediately upon his conversion, Alypius having been converted, too, Augustine went with his friend to Monica. He exclaims to God: "You turned her mourning into a joy far richer than she had desired, far dearer and purer than that she had sought in grandchildren born of my flesh."[7]

As a footnote it must be noted that Augustine's father played a considerably smaller and in some ways negative role in Augustine's movement toward faith. His father was baptized only on his death bed, and Augustine says of his mother Monica: "For she strove in every way that you, my God, would be my father rather than he. In this you aided her, so that she overcame her husband, to whom she, the better partner, was subject. For in this she assuredly was serving you who ordered her to do so."[8]

While Monica and her training and prayers were undoubtedly the primary scurce which helped prepare Augustine for his conversion, four other influences should be mentioned as well— Augustine's love of philosophy, Ambrose, Augustine's friends, and the workings of providence.

From early on Augustine was clearly possessed with a lively intellect and an eagerness to find a philosophy which would put the world into perspective. Indeed, his conversion to Christianity was not his first conversion. Busy in his quest after career and knowledge in Carthage, Augustine found Cicero: "In the ordinary course of study I came upon a book by a certain Cicero, whose tongue almost all men admire but not his heart. This work contains his exhortation to philosophy and is called *Hortensius*. This book changed my affections. It turned my prayers to you, Lord, and caused me to have different purposes and desires. All my vain hopes forthwith became worthless to me, and with incredible ardor of heart I desired undying wisdom . . . How I burned, 0 my God, how I burned with desire to fly away from earthly things and upwards to you. . . . "9

The quest for wisdom led Augustine in a different direction than it had led Cicero. With his Christian heritage he sought some way to combine the quest for truth and light with Christian stories and the Bible. He found such a combination on the next stage of his intellectual journey—Manicheism. For nine years Augustine was a "hearer" among the Manichees—not a full convert but a fellow-traveler. The dualism they drew between divine forces of good and divine forces of evil spoke to his own divided soul, and he tried to discover through reason a pure self to which he could cling. Like many "cults" today which attract searching and uncertain young people, the Manichees were rigorous in their demands and popular with youth in part because established society found them so unattractive.

In Milan, just before his conversion, Augustine found in platonism a new clue to true wisdom. Now he no longer sought the Manichean God within, but a transcendent God beyond the temporal world, dwelling in eternal light with the eternal Son: "Being thus admonished to return to myself, under your leadership (0 God) I entered into my inmost being. . . . I entered there, and by my soul's eye, such as it was, I saw above that same eye of my soul, above my mind, an unchangeable light. . . . It was above my mind, because it made me. . . . Love knows it, 0 eternal truth, and true love, and beloved eternity! You are my God, and I sigh for you day and night!"10

Augustine's search for a mediator between that Light and his own life helped prepare the way for his conversion to Catholic Christianity.

Augustine was not only led toward Christian faith by his love of philosophy. He was led also by the influence of Ambrose, the Bishop of Milan. Ambrose was an ally with Monica in hoping for

Augustine's conversion. He mas himself an orator of such persuasive power that Augustine coveted Ambrose's gift. Like Augustine, Ambrose had been influenced by platonic thought and therefore he could speak to Augustine's philosophical concerns. Ambrose clearly touched Augustine in that special way that only true mentora, models and heroes can do: "I came to Milan, and to Ambrose, its bishop, a man famed throughout the world as one of its very best men, and your devout worshiper. By his eloquent sermons in those days he zealously provided your people with the fat of your wheat, the gladness of your oil, and the sobering intoxication of your wine. All unknowing, I was led to him by you, so that through him I might be led, while fully knowing it, to you."[11]

A third influence leading Augustine to his conversion was his love for his friends. One's sense is that Augustine was a person eager to love, needing to love, and finding in human relationships not quite that perfect love for which he longed.

Of the death of a friend of his youth he writes: "My heart was made dark by sorrow, and whatever I looked upon was death. My native place was a torment to me, and my father's house a strange unhappiness. Whatsoever I had done together with him was, apart from him, turned into a cruel torture. My eyes sought for him on every side, and he was not given to them. I hated all things, because they no longer held him."[12]

Of the loss of his concubine, Augustine writes: "The woman with whom I was wont to share my bed was torn from my side as an impediment to my marriage. My heart still clung to her: it was pierced and wounded within me, and the wound drew blood from it."[13]

Looking back on the loss of his friend, Augustine suggests that the imperfection of human loves helped drive him toward the love of God: "But blessed is the man who loves you, and his friend in you, and his enemy for your sake. For he alone loses no dear one to whom all are dear in him who is not lost. But who is this unless our God? . . . "[14]

Finally, Augustine can look back on his life and see how the leading of Providence helped bring him to his conversion. (Indeed, he would see every influence as the outworking of God's providential care.)

Looking back on the pear which he stole for the pleasure of stealing, and not because he needed the pear itself, Augustine shows a lively sense of sin: "Foul was the evil, and I loved it. I loved to go down to death. I loved my fault, not that for which I did the fault, but I loved my fault itself."[15]

Furthermore, it turns out that just about the time of his conversion, Augustine's skill as an orator was marred by some physical infirmity. He was having to prepare to give up his chosen career, and this troubled him greatly. Was this part of the preparation for his conversion, too?[16]

Of course Augustine's pilgrimage does not end with the voice in the garden and the reading of the text from Romans. He moves from rhetorician to cleric to bishop, from philosopher to Christian philosopher and *The City of God*. But the heart of what we learn from Augustine's story is this: The moment of conversion and decision is the culmination of a process that began from the womb. That process was worked out through the example, nagging, and prayers of Monica; through Augustine's intellectual quest for true wisdom; through the preaching and example of Ambrose; through the love for others which led finally to the love for God. Through all these influences, Augustine was brought to the point where he could hear, "Take and read," and opening the Scriptures could know that the words he read were addressed to him, and that the light he had sought would now illumine his own soul.

II.

Dorothy Day was the primary founder and leading spirit of the Catholic Worker Movement in the United States. She serves as an example of the lively relationship between Christian faith and social concern.

Like Augustine, Dorothy Day lived with the prayer to be released from her unacceptable life—only not yet. And like Augustine she moved toward conversion, though her conversion was neither so dramatic nor so conclusive as his.

As Augustine had been living with his concubine, so Dorothy Day was living with her common-law husband, Forster Batterham. Dorothy was interested in becoming a Christian and a Catholic. Forster had no interest in being either one. A child was due, and Dorothy began to know that she would want the child baptized. Forster opposed all such ceremonies and bonds. For Dorothy to choose the church would be to let her husband go.

As with Augustine, the human love Dorothy felt, in this case for her newborn daughter, compelled her to seek an even deeper and eternal love: "No human creature could receive or contain so vast a flood of love and joy as I often felt after the birth of my child. With this came the need to worship, to adore."[17]

Dorothy writes of the first months of her daughter's life: "I read *The Imitation of Christ* a great deal during those months. I knew that I was going to have my child baptized, cost what it may. I knew that I was not going to have her floundering through many years as I had done, doubting and hesitating, undisciplined and amoral. I felt it was the greatest thing I could do for my child. For myself, I prayed the gift of faith. I was sure, yet not sure. I postponed the day of decision."[18]

Soon Dorothy could postpone her commitment no longer. Her daughter, Tamar, was baptized and then not long after, Dorothy, too. There were no angels visitant, no opening skies: "The next day I went to Tottenville alone, leaving Tamar with my sister, and there with Sister Aloysia as my godparent, I was baptized conditionally, since I had already been baptized in the Episcopal Church. I made my first confession right afterward, and looked forward the next morning to receiving communion.

"I had no particular joy in partaking of these three sacraments, Baptism, Penance and Holy Eucharist. I proceeded about my own active participation in them grimly, coldly, making acts of faith, and certainly with no consolation whatever. One part of my mind stood at one side and kept saying: What are you doing?"[19]

Dorothy's description of her younger self is "doubting, hesitating, undisciplined and amoral." This may seem to critics less harsh than herself to be overstated. What is clear is that though she came from a home with considerable affection, particularly on her mother's side, no great guiding force like Monica propelled her safely toward the church.

"All of my life I have been haunted by God," she said. "How much did I hear of religion as a child? Very little, and yet my heart leaped when I heard the name of God."[20]

There was little formal religion at home. There was an

acknowledgment of God's existence. There were reminders of right and wrong. One gets the sense that Dorothy, rather than being surrounded by piety, had her own innate piety and had to seek out sources to sustain it.

"In Oakland," Dorothy says,"(I was eight then) we lived next door to a Methodist family who had a little store with a tiny apartment in back. The entire place smelled of fresh shingles. Birdie, my neighbor, took me to Sunday sohool and church with her, and then I began to experience real piety, in the sense of the sweetness of faith. I believed, but I did not know in what I believed."[21]

In Chicago, Dorothy surprised a Catholic neighbor, Mrs. Barrett, in her prayers: "I felt a burst of love toward Mrs. Barrett that I have never forgotten, a feeling of gratitude and happiness that warmed my heart."[22]

Then Dorothy found the Episcopal church at 35th and Cottage Grove and, like Augustine, she became a catechumen, and as with him, nothing came of it for a very long time.

Along with this innate piety, there was another strain in Dorothy—her longing for social justice, her compassion for the dispossessed of the world. That passion was growing stronger and stronger when she went away to the University of Illinois. It got her arrested in women's causes, gave her the impetus for her later jobs with Socialist papers, allied her with many in New York and Chicago who were working toward a new vision of America and of the world, a vision to be realized through revolution.

In that milieu of revolutionary fervor Dorothy fell in love and had an affair that helped her know the depth of longing and the depth of her disappointment, too. Her book *The Long Loneliness* does not refer to that affair, but its title may in part reflect it.[23]

Again among those seeking social justice, Dorothy found Forster Batterham, who became her common-law husband. She bore her daughter, Tamar, and found in Tamar both the longing and the joy which helped hring her to her unenthusiastic baptism and to the Catholic Church.

Her biographer, William D. Miller, writes of the relationship between Dorothy's baptism and her longing for social justice: "Over the years, though, her radical friends—or many of them at least—seemed to be more comfortable with her conversion than did many of her co-religionists, who were staunch defenders of the values of bourgeoisity. As her radical friends seemed to appreciate, conversion had not lessened her passion for a better world; it had started her along the path toward a vision they had shared, no matter what they called it or how they defined it. Both Dorothy and her radical friends were seeking community, the final and complete harmonization of all. The difference was that her friends talked of this goal as something that would crown their revolutionary struggle—that would be found in time. But for Dorothy, as she came to see, the way was love and the end was eternity."[24]

There was formal Christian education leading to Dorothy's baptism, instruction in catechism which she does not describe winsomely: "Three times a week, Sister Aloysia came to give me a catechism lesson, which I dutifully tried to learn. But she insisted that I recite word for word with the repetition of the question that was in the book. If I had not learned my lesson she rebuked me. 'And you think that you are intelligent!' she would say witheringly, 'My fourth-grade pupils know more than you do!'

"I hadn't a doubt but that they did. I struggled on day by day, learning without question. I was in an agreeable and lethargic— almost bovine state of mind."[25]

As for her social passion and its relationship to faith, Dorothy says that at her baptism she knew nothing of the social teaching of the church. She had her social passion on the one hand and her love for Tamar and for God on the other. Conversion had come, but crucial nurture was to follow.

Here is how Dorothy Day writes of the periods of her life. "My life has been divided into two parts. The first twenty-five years were floundering, years of joy and sorrow, it is true, but certainly with a sense of that insecurity one hears so much about these days. I did not know in what I believed, though I tried to serve a cause. Five years after I became a Catholic I met Peter Maurin and his story must play a great part in this work because he was my master and I was his disciple."[26]

In this version, at least, the great turning point is not Dorothy's conversion, but her friendship with Peter.

The story of Peter Maurin is given in *The Long Loneliness*, and much of his philosophy is found in *Loaves and Fishes*.

He was an unlikely immigrant from France, living perhaps in deliberate poverty, though it is not altogether clear that he could

48

have earned much of a living had he tried. He found in Dorothy the disciple he needed. She had the gift of enfleshing his ideas and turning his words into practical action.

To the more objective observer—to us reading Dorothy's work and hearing of Peter's words, it is not at all clear that the disciple was not above the master. It may well be that Dorothy's intelligence and imagination drew more wisdom from Peter Maurin than strictly speaking was there. But there can be no doubt that she regarded him as teacher, catalyst, and. for her, representative of God.

In Peter's "personalism," which sought to see what was godly in every person and called every person to assert her or his own worth, Dorothy found a Christianity that could embrace love of God and social justice. Her compassion for people, her pacifism, and her loyalty to the church as the locus for personalism, found inspiration and warrant in Peter Maurin.

One piece of Peter's teaching gives a sense of his ideas and his style. It is called "A Case for Utopia."

The world would be better off
if people tried to become better, and people would become better
if they stopped trying to become better off.
For when everyone tries to become
better off
nobody is better off.
But when everyone tries to become better everybody is
better off.
Everyone would be rich
if nobody tried to become richer,
and nobody would be poor
if everybody tried to be the poorest
And everybody would be what he ought to be
if everybody tried to be
what he wants the other fellow to be.[27]

Surely Dorothy's long loneliness found its beginning and its solution in God, but no one reading her words on Peter can doubt that he was an instrument of God's compassion to her. As

Monica nurtured Augustine toward conversion, Peter Maurin nurtured Dorothy Day from conversion. These two mentors, we would think, nourished Christians more remarkable than themselves, but that is not a bad occupation for saints.

III.

Because the purpose of this discussion is to foster reflection on our own journeys, our own mix of nurture and commitment, I turn from stellar examples of the Christian life to a far more modest illustration, myself.

As we recalled Augustine's baptism and Dorothy Day's, I now recall my own. I was baptized at almost twelve years of age in the First Baptist Church of Evanston, Illinois. I was baptized by my father, the pastor of that church, in an evening service on Palm Sunday. It is common among Baptists to doubt, not the efficacy, but the significance of our baptism. While we believe in believers' baptism, we note that most of us come to our decision just about as we reach puberty and as our friends are either being confirmed or having their Bar or Bat Mitzvahs. For me, however, the baptism marked a genuine decision, the culmination of twelve years of modest piety seeking some proper object. I have never thought that it was too soon, too little, or too perfunctory to count.

It is perhaps not coincidental that I found my baptism significant *and* that I was baptized by my father. The Apostle Paul firmly denies that *who* baptizes you matters at all. He insists that it is being baptized into Christ rather than being baptized by Paul or Apollos that counts. I know how theologically correct that is, but for a twelve-year-old whose father had also been his pastor, preacher, friend, and teacher of the candidates' class, *who* did the baptizing did make a difference.

Baptism became a symbol not only of my decision for Jesus but of the influences that had led me to that decision. My father, who baptized me, was a symbol for my family. The church in which I was baptized was a reminder of the community of faith which sustained me on my journey to that moment.

Faith, hope, and love were realities in my home before I knew the words for them. They were not so much talked about as expressed. And they were not expressed perfectly, but for a twelve-year-old they were as near perfection as anyone could wish. In the affirmation lived out by my parents, by my grandmothers, who often lived with us, in the daily give and take with my brothers and sisters—where whatever else we doubted we never doubted that we were loved and loved fully—I glimpsed something of the biblical notion of community and saw through a glass darkly that love which, Paul insists, we shall one day see face to face.

Someone caught the image of driving home late at night from some occasion—a movie, say, or a ballgame—your parents talking quietly in the front seat and you half dozing in back, believing that you are perfectly loved and perfectly safe—a lost Eden for which we all long. It was something like that.

There was the further advantage that when I attended church, I heard my father put words to the experiences we knew at home. In the pulpit he was and is articulate and winsome, speaking of God, love, loyalty, trust, and faith. So it was that unlike many children I not only had the reality of Christian nurture, I had an interpreter, and the interpreter was one of my prime nurturers. My mother, whose role in all this I have come to appreciate more deeply with the years, interpreted less but provided equally for our nurture—and heaven knows, of my father's.

And there was the church. As have my children now, I had from my first memory a host of courtesy aunts and uncles, grandmothers and grandfathers. I stuffed myself at church suppers, played hide and seek in odd corners of the educational wing, and found myself wrapped in church as if it were the air I breathed. There was little sentimentality in my attachment to the church. I knew that the church in which I was baptized had fought over whether to admit black people to membership. I knew that Mrs. Doe, who sat teary-eyed during prayer meeting, was teary-eyed because Mr. Doe, a deacon, had run off with his secretary. I discovered later in seminary that those students who were disillusioned with the church were those who had not grown up in its bosom. I had few illusions to start with. But the nourishment was there.

Finally, in regard to my preparation for baptism that Palm Sunday, I must say that I remember my church school teachers fairly vividly, but not one word they said. Curriculum always seemed a little too sweet for my taste—I early loved *Treasure Island, Robin Hood*, and *The Black Stallion*—and the moral solutions seemed a little too easy. For the teachers themselves I have only praise. I assume they loved Jesus. I know they loved us, which was not always easy to do.

If my baptism represented my first conversion, there was a second conversion to come. In the years between, however, education, nurture, was more the mode of my pilgrimage than conversion and decision. Faith was seeking understanding, not always without pain.

In the new church to which we moved in Los Angeles, I was happy in finding friends, sometimes friends who were accepting and kind when school was harder, more competitive, more harsh. I was also influenced—blessed—by two ministers to youth who modeled for me faith which was both committed and thoughtful. They gave me books to read, ideas to play with. They introduced me to Paul Tillich, who, for whatever reasons, meant more to me in late adolescence than he has since. The support I found in church gave me increased confidence in other areas, and by the time I left for college, I felt accepted and affirmed in school as well as church. I had (sounding now like St. Paul, boasting so as to present my fall) done well academically and in student government. I felt like the King of the Mountain.

To college then I came, where a host of other kings and queens from their own mountains had come. The competition was fierce. Self-confidence began to wane. If I was not what I had been, what of the supports that had surrounded me? Were they as illusory as my superior gifts?

The first blow as I moved toward my fall, was delivered by Michael Scriven, a professor of philosophy and an atheist in the way Billy Graham is a Christian—fervently. The rumor around the Common Room, passed on to fearful freshmen, was that the Scriven grading system vorked thus: A for atheists, B for Buddhists, C for Christians, and F for fundamentalists.

Class with Mr. Scriven was a grueling, battering experience. Walking one night with my father, seeking to explain the problems of college philosophy, I came to my solution of the moment, though not a novel solution, "You have to do it all on faith," I said, "blind faith, with no reasoning mixed in to confuse the issue."

"I still think," said my father, "that we've got a quart and a half of reality. And our Christian faith is like a quart bottle. You can't get everything in, but it's the best bottle I know to make the best sense we can."

That helped me get through freshman year. Sophomore year was worse. The reasons are perhaps worth analysis and psycho-analysis, but I shall spare us all. What confidence I had left was even further shattered, and I was left as a deposed King of the Mountain, with no more powers at my command.

Reading one night a book given me by one of those ministers to youth I have mentioned, I came across a sentence which I have never found in that book since: "You are not asked to be sufficient." (Did the children playing next to Augustine's garden really say, "Take up and read," or did he hear what he needed to hear? Did Peter Maurin give Dorothy Day the vision or did he unlock the vision hidden in her heart?) Whatever the book really said, I heard it say: "You are not asked to be sufficient."

Now for the first and definitive time, God's general goodness turned into God's specific grace and began to show itself in the face of Jesus Christ. This newer faith still sought understanding. Seminary helped, sometimes despite itself. St. Paul, whom I had always avoided in favor of the Gospels, became and is still the central interpreter of gospel, good news, for me. Karl Barth, whom I had avoided while seeking that Ultimate Concern lined out by Tillich, showed me concerns more ultimate yet and named these as incarnate in Jesus Christ—perhaps a little less incarnate, flesh and blood, sweat and tears than I would wish. But Barth marked another turning point.

Along with these thinkers, Calvary Baptist Church became central to my life. Its building has now become the Yale Repertory Theater, which is appropriate, since my pastor and boss of those years was the most dramatic and peripatetic preacher I have known. Calvary was a dying church which after twenty-three years is still dying, quite healthily. That congregation provided what my faith had started with and needed still: community.

In those years I began the most important Christian education of my life. I started preaching: once a month then, now once a week. I was given the gift of wrestling with the texts and the commentaries and the lives of the people of God.

The rest we pass through quickly but gratefully. My vocation has consisted of a mix of seminary teaching and preaching, educating and proclaiming, constantly needing to reaffirm my own conviction and hoping to draw forth conviction from others.

I spent almost as long a stretch teaching and preaching at Chicago as I did at Yale. It was like a second graduate education, with all Chicago's modern and post-modern questions alive and well. How does Christ speak to culture? What can we say to those who have not stepped into the circle of belief?

In those years came also the gift of a wife and children, who for me have become central to my understanding of who God is and what God asks, and who are a constant education.

In 1981 I moved to my present parish, whose great gift and challenge and threat is that we really do try to show forth the multiplicity of the family of God—in race, in theology, in marital status, in age, in lifestyle.

I did not know when I stood in the lukewarm water, held by my father's arms, and said; "I do accept Jesua Christ as my Lord and Savior, and I will follow him all my days," that where he would lead would be to that odd, awkward, gracious church in Oakland.

But looking back on the journey, I am glad.

The Journey in Our History

by David L. Bartlett

The tension between conversion and nurture, commitment and growth is as old as the Christian community. I want to use some classic examples to suggest the depth of the tension between conversion and nurture but also to suggest that from the beginning of Christian history there has been a movement toward mutual enrichment. Commitment and growth feed and nourish one another.

I.

In the world of the New Testament we can already see the tension between those communities and books which stress evangelism and those communities and books which stress education and catechesis. To oversimplify, in the beginning of the church, under the pressure of the coming kingdom, biblical writers stressed evangelism, conversion and, implicitly, church growth. As the community settled in for the long haul of history, the movement was more toward education and nurture, passing on the content of the faith to succeeding generations.

A classic example of the movement from crisis to education is found in the movement from Paul's letters to the pastoral epistles—1 and 2 Timothy and Titus. (My own conviction is that Paul did not write the pastorals but that they are the product of a later generation of Christians. However, the same comparison can be made even if we assume the the pastoral represent Paul's last writings, some time after the crisis and expectation of, say, the Corinthian letters.)

Nothing is more obvious than that Paul writes such letters as 1 and 2 Corinthians and Galatians under the pressure of the kingdom which is coming and which has already broken in, in the coming of Jesus Christ.

> For the love of Christ controls us, because we are convinced that one has died for all, therefore all have died. And he died for all, that those who live might live no longer for themselves but for him who for their sake died and was raised.
> From now on, therefore, we regard no one from a human point of view; even though we once regarded Christ from a human point of view, we regard him thus no longer. Therefore, for any one who is in Christ, there is a new creation, the old has passed away, behold, the new has come. All this is from God, who through Christ reconciled us to himself and gave us the ministry of reconciliation. . . . So we are ambassadors for Christ, God making his appeal through us. We beseech you on behalf of Christ, be reconciled to God. (2 Corinthians 5:14-20, RSV emended by the author.)

The New Age, the kingdom for which faithful people have waited is about to reach its fullness and indeed has begun in Jesus Christ, who is the firstfruits of the resurrection of all faithful people. In Jesus Christ, we see both the conviction of sin and the promise of reconciliation. The purpose of preaching, of apostleship, and we may say of Christian testimony is to state the imperative which is also a comfort: "Be reconciled to God."

Another text which obviously shows forth the urgency of the time comes from Paul's first letter to the church at Corinth:

> When I came to you, brothers and sisters, I did not come proclaiming to you the testimony of God in lofty words of wisdom. For I decided to know nothing among you except Jesus Christ and him crucified. And I was with you in weakness and in much fear and trembling, and my speech and my message were not in plausible words of wisdom, but in demonstration of the Spirit and of power, that your faith might not rest in human wisdom, but in the power of God. (1 Corinthians 2:1-5, RSV emended by the author.)

Here we sense the urgency of the message, the central emphasis on faith as commitment to the crucified Lord. The inbreaking of God's Spirit in power and grace.

Yet even within Paul, who feels the pull of God's inbreaking kingdom and preaches the gospel for the sake of commitment, change, redemption, there is a balance to be struck. Life in the new age still touches on life in the age which is passing away. The gospel opens a new creation, but it does not end responsibility. There is the responsibility for nurture, thought, ethical growth, even for Christian people who have received the new life in Christ.

We can perhaps demonstrate the Pauline tension by showing his major concerns in two of his epistles. To put the issue in our terms, Paul writes 1 Corinthians to a church that has celebrated conversion without education and nurture. He writes Galatians to a church where education and rules have been divorced from good news, from gospel, from new life and conversion.

Early on in 1 Corinthians, Paul makes clear to these Christians that they have miles to go before they sleep, or are resurrected, either one:

> But I, brothers and sisters, could not address you as spiritual people, but as people of the flesh, as babes in Christ. I fed you with milk, not solid food; for you were not ready for it; and even yet you are not ready. (1 Corinthians 3:1-2, RSV emended.)

The unreadiness of the Corinthians, as I read it, consists especially in their sense that they are absolutely ready. They believe that in their conversion and receiving of the Spirit they received all the gifts that they need for the fullness of life here and hereafter. They believe that their conversion and their baptism have moved them into the realm of resurrection and that is all they know or need to know—all they need to do. So a few verses later on Paul characterizes their religious self-esteem: "Already you are filled! Already you have become rich! Without us you have become kings! And would that you did reign, so that we might share the rule with you!" (1 Corinthians 4:8). The sarcasm is obvious.

The consequence of the Corinthians' fervent and whole-hearted conversion, of the sense that they've got all they need, is that the Corinthians do not think that they need nurture in either morality or responsibility. They have the love of Jesus down in their hearts, and with that going for them, nothing can faze them, "All things are lawful for me!" they say, perhaps quoting Paul back to himself. He responds with concern for what Christian nurture ought to teach them: "'All things are lawful for me,' but not all things are helpful, 'All things are lawful for me,' but I will not be enslaved by anything" (1 Corinthians 6:12).

The Corinthians seek salvation without consequences. Freed from bondage to sin (as he believes), one of them enters into an incestuous relationship, and the others applaud his bravery. The Corinthian men visit houses of prostitution and see no conflict between that conduct and their baptism. Wealthy Corinthians come to the communion meal early, pulling the pate and cabernet out of their baskets, and by the time the poor arrive from their daily chores, the wealthy are drunk and out of food. "All things are lawful."

The first letter to the Corinthians is itself a classic example of Christian education. Paul insists that the Corinthians' faith should seek understanding and that their freedom should issue in responsibility.

As faithful people they need to understand the great "not yet" of Paul's gospel. The resurrection has begun, but it is not yet complete, and in the meantime they live in hope, not by sight. As responsible people they need to understand the limitations of freedom: "Love is patient and kind; love is not jealous or boastful. . . . Love does not insist on its own way" (1 Corinthians 13:4-5).

We find in this epistle Paul, the educator *par excellence*:

> For though you have countless guides in Christ, you do not have many fathers. For I became your father in Christ Jesus, through the gospel. I urge you, therefore, be imitators of me. (1 Corinthians 4:15-16)

The Galatians end up on the other horn of the dilemma; or they collapse the tension in the other direction—what you will. They become increasingly concerned for appropriate practice— what does the Lord require of us? And they reach some conclusions: circumcision for the males; certain feast days or fasting days for all; we do not know for sure the rest.

We sense tbat a certain kind of ethical instruction has gone well—and too well—among the Galatians. They have discovered what they are supposed to do, and with other Christians since who believe in the rightness of their own practices, they are insisting that other Christians do exactly the same. All men must be circumcised. All Christians observe these feasts. That is what we have been taught, so it must hold good for you as well.

Paul, who thinks the Corinthians have too much spirit and too much freedom, thinks that the Galatians have lost both. Bound by the rules they have learned, they forget the Spirit which guides them. Driven to perform according to the standards they are taught, they are forgetting the liberty of Christians who live by the outpouring of God's grace:

> Formerly, when you did not know God, you were in bondage to beings that by nature are no gods; but now that you have come to know God, or rather to be known by God, how can you turn back again to the weak and beggarly elemental spirits, whose slaves you want to be once more? You observe days, and months, and seasons, and years! I am afraid I have labored over you in vain. (Galatians 4:8-11)

> For freedom Christ has set us free; stand fast therefore, and do not submit again to a yoke of slavery. Now I, Paul, say to you that if you receive circumcision, Christ will be of no advantage to you. (Galatians 5:1-2)

> O foolish Galatians! . . . Let me ask you only this: Did you receive the Spirit by works of the law, or by hearing with faith? (Galatians 3:1-2)

Of course Paul is still worried that once they find their freedom again, the Galatians may act like the Corinthians and give everything over to the flesh. Thus we have the reminder in Galatians 5 that the true fruits of the Spirit are responsibility and not libertinism.

I have argued elsewhere that Paul, for all his eschatological fervor, is an excellent model both for conversion and for Christian education precisely because he shows us that faithful education lives under eschatological zeal.[1]

Nonetheless, if we were to set him as a model for our concerns, we should set him as the model of the one saved by grace, preaching grace so that others might receive the gracious word through faith and live it as citizens of a new creation.

Within the new creation there is need for nurture and structure, but the structure, the rules, the practices, the teachings should not—must not—be allowed to replace the working of the Spirit.

With the pastoral epistles we enter another world. Whether it is a world later in Paul's ministry or a world later than Paul's ministry there is much dispute. I believe the pastorals were written after Paul's death, but nothing in this discussion hangs on that belief.

For whatever reason, the eschatalogical tension is reduced. The church will be around for a while to come, and nurture becomes the center of concern more than conversion.

As is often the case in the church's history, the pressure of heresy makes it essential to the writer that right teaching be established in the church and among its members. Paul is now seen not so much as apostle, evangelist, and preacher but as a teacher who passes on sound doctrine to Timothy and Titus, who in turn are to pass that sound doctrine on to their congregations.

Sound doctrine always issues in virtuous practice. Those who rightly understand the faith live upright and exemplary lives. The guarantee that doctrine will be sound and conduct will be virtuous comes through the succession of Christian teachers. They themselves must be qualified to teach by the excellence of their lives. By implication, at least, they stand in a kind of succession of right teaching and right living, passed on from Paul to Timothy and Titus, to the generation for which the pastorals were written.

Jesus' dealing with humankind is represented by his two appearances, or epiphanies. In the first epiphany, Jesus came to establish the standards of virtue and right teaching. (The picture of Jesus as a guarantor of right teaching has often appealed to a strain of Christian educators as central to their understanding of Christ.) In the second epiphany, the final coming, now indefinitely delayed, Christ will return to judge Christians on how faithful they have been to those virtues he taught.[2]

Perhaps we can get a sense of the concerns of the pastoral epistles by presenting a kind of collage of the themes we have suggested:

Paul, an apostle of Christ Jesus by command of our

God and Savior and of Christ Jesus our hope,

To Timothy, my true child in the faith [not in faith but in *the* faith]. . . .

As I urged you when I was going to Macedonia, remain at Ephesus, that you may charge certain persons not to teach any different doctrine. (1 Timothy 1:1-3)

I desire that in every place men should pray, lifting holy hands without anger or quarreling, also that women should adorn themselves modestly and sensibly in seemly apparel, not with braided hair or gold or pearls or costly attire but by good deeds, as befits women who profess religion. (1 Timothy 2:8-10)

Now a bishop must be above reproach, the husband of one wife, temperate, sensible, dignified, hospitable, an apt teacher, no drunkard, not violent but gentle, not quarrelsome, and no lover of money. He must manage his own household well, keeping his children submissive and respectful in every way; for if a man does not know how to manage his own household, how can he care for God's church? (1 Timothy 3:2-5)

If you put these instructions before the brethren, you will be a good minister of Christ Jesus, nourished in the words of the faith and of the good doctrine which you have followed. (1 Timothy 4:6)

For the grace of God has appeared for the salvation of all people, training us to renounce irreligion and worldly passions, and to live sober, upright and godly lives in this world, awaiting our blessed hope, the appearing of the glory of our great God and Savior Jesus Christ, who gave himself for us to redeem us from all iniquity and to purify himself a people of his own who are zealous for good deeds. (Titus 2:11-14)

We must add that, in the pastorals, the faith is not only passed on by official teachers of the church; it is also passed on within the family. The author writes Timothy: "I am reminded of your sincere faith, a faith that dwelt first in your grandmother Lois and your mother Eunice and now, I am sure, dwells in you." Paul's role is not to provide faith but to rekindle that faith Timothy has received from his grandmother and mother. "Hence I remind you to rekindle the gift of God that is within you by the laying on of hands" (2 Timothy 1:5-6). Of this familial faith, Horace Bushnell, whom we shall soon discuss, says much.

We see, then, that because Paul, or the early Paul, lives with the sense of the kingdom coming and already come, the stress is on conversion and commitment. Yet even within this framework there is concern for nurture, ethical living, responsibility. There is a tension between the zeal of faith and the practice of faithfulness.

With the pastorals, the urgency of initial commitment has faded, and the issue is how to preserve, not faith, but *the* faith. Faithful life is no longer life in the Spirit, but life according to the virtues. The church is less the eschatalogical community and more an institution with established offices and officers, and the role of officers is in part to impart correct teaching over against heresy.

(We move for a moment to our time. Is there still a sense in which eschatalogical zeal leads appropriately to the stress on evangelism, while outside heretical threats and institutional needs point to the stress on education and structure? Is our contemporary "church growth" movement—which I support—nevertheless an old mix? Does it proclaim on the one hand zeal for the gospel but reflect on the other hand institutional anxiety, as our familiar structures lose ground both to more "evangelical" bodies and to the secular world?

(Or put another way, do we confuse the times? Do we turn and return to structures and institutions as if this were any old time, instead of proclaiming the good news in the eager awareness that the kingdom is even now breaking in? Who reads our age, John XXIII calling for fresh air, or John Paul II scurrying to close the windows?)

II.

We move from Christian origins, from the New Testament, to origins in the New World. I am not an historian, much less an historian of American religious history, so rather than trace large movements I have chosen to look at two paradigmatic figures— Jonathan Edwards and Horace Bushnell. I choose them in part because they interest me. I choose them in part because they are influential mediators between the New Testament church and our own churches.

Put briefly, Edwards is the great American paradigm of evangelism, conversion, and commitment. He is certainly the most sophisticated thinker and profound meditator on the nature of such commitment that the American church has produced. Horace Bushnell is the founding father of Christian education, a man with remarkable insights into the formative aspects of the faith—and into the developmental possibilities of children.

Each of them reflects the historical context in which he writes. Edwards, like Paul, wrote at a time of eschatological excitement. Bushnell, as with the pastorals, wrote when the American experiment and the American churches were apparently here to stay. Each of them has more balance and diversity than any quick study of their views would suggest.

In what follows I draw primarily on Edwards' *A Treatise Concerning Religious Affections* and on Bushnell's *Christian Nurture*.

It would be overly simple to suggest that Jonathan Edwards, like the Apostle Paul, lived in a time rampant with apocalyptic expectation. However, though Edwards did not stress the impending end of history, in broader terms his preaching and his concerns were eschatological. Everyone stood in the face of judgment day. God would bring the elect into a right relationship with God's self. It was the appropriate time to repent.

Closely related to our concern for the relationship between evangelism and education, was Edwards' unhappiness with allowing children and young people who had not themselves had a clear sign of saving experience full membership and communicant status in the church. Edwards served in Northampton, Massachusetts. His intransigence on this and other issues led to his dismissal from that parish after twenty-three years. In 1750 he preached his farewell sermon to that congregation before heading west to Stockbridge and a ministry to Indians. Among the admonitions in his moving farewell sermon were these words to the children of the congregation, words which suggest precisely what a century later Bushnell strove to overcome:

> Dear children, . . . some of you, sometimes, have seemed to be affected with what I have said to you. But I am afraid it has had no saving effect, as to many of you; but that you remain still in an unconverted condition, without any real saving work wrought in your souls, convincing you thoroughly of your sin and misery, causing you to see the great evil of sin, and to mourn for it, and

hate it above all things . . . so that I now leave you in a miserable condition, having no interest in Christ, and so under the awful displeasure and anger of God, and in danger of going down to the pit of eternal misery.[3]

Four years before, in 1746, Edwards had published *A Treatise Concerning Religious Affections*, his final and most impressive attempt to account for, validate, and test the Great Awakening, that remarkable time of fervor and conversion which had as one of its starting points that same church in Northampton which in 1750 decided to let Edwards go.

The book is in part a defense of the affections as being central to the religious life. It is not primarily reason, but affection, longing, loving, willing which leads men and women to true religion and a right relationship with God. Edwards does not, however, undervalue reason. His description of the religious affections is a remarkable mix of scriptural interpretation and metaphysics. It is a highly reasoned defense of the primacy of the affections.

Central to Edwards' view of the religious affections is the claim that at the time of conversion God gives to the new believer a new sense, a new power within the soul. It is this sense, and not our natural senses or our imagination, through which God communicates truth to the believer. Or perhaps more accurately, it is through this sense that God communicates God's self to the believer, while the believer is drawn to the beauty of God.

The bulk of the *Treatise*, however, is not written to defend the affections as central to true piety. The bulk is written to show the signs of genuine religious affections, so that real conversion might be separated from false conversion and true faith known as true faith. It is here that one finds hints of Edwards' sense of the role of Christian nurture in the life of true piety. On the one hand there is the suggestion that conversion does not come all at once, but begins in modest ways. On the other hand there is the clear claim that, beyond the moment of conversion, Christian believers are called to grow in the depth and practice of their faith.

When Edwards writes about the Fourth Sign of true religious affections, he suggests that when conversion begins it begins in so modest a degree that full awakening is far from realized:

And were it not for the very imperfect degree, in which

[the spiritual] sense is commonly given at first, or the small degree of this glorious light that first dawns upon the soul; the change made by this spiritual opening of the eyes in conversion, would be much greater, and more remarkable, every way, than if a man, who had been born blind . . . should continue so for a long time, and then at once should have the sense of seeing imparted to him.[4]

(Another hint of the relationship between nurture and full awakening comes not from Edwards' writings but from his life and is found in two suggestions made by Sydney Ahlstrom: "Both [Edwards'] parents were persons of rare endowments, deeply concerned for the liberal education and spiritual nurture of their children."[5] And, suggests Ahlstrom, Edwards' freedom from concern over certain technical questions regarding clerical authority: "Perhaps . . . testifies to the fine example and nurture provided by his father, who had not sacrificed the affective dimensions of the Christian faith to the aridities of dogma and politics."[6])

What is very evident in Edwards' work is his concern for growth following conversion. Indeed, one way to read his discussion of the twelve signs of true religious affections is to suggest that Edwards insists on true growth in grace and suggests that those who hold to the ecstasy or memory of their first conversion as the only sign of their salvation are not really regenerate at all.

Edwards claims that the true convert grows in understanding:

Holy affections are not heat without light; but evermore arise from some information of the understanding, some spiritual instruction that the mind receives, some light or actual knowledge. . . . Knowledge is the key that first opens the hard heart and enlarges the affections, and so opens the way for men into the kingdom of heaven.[7]

The true convert grows in the struggle against sin:

But many in these days have got into a strange antiscriptural way, of having all their striving and wrestling over before they are converted; and so having an easy time of it afterwards, to sit down and enjoy their sloth and indolence.[8]

The true convert grows in living the Christlike life:

Truly gracious affections differ from those affections that are false and delusive, in that they tend to, and are attended with the lamblike, dovelike spirit and temper of Jesus Christ; or in other words, they naturally beget and promote such a spirit of love, meekness, quietness, forgiveness and mercy, as appeared in Christ.[9]

The true convert never rests:

And a transformation of nature is continued and carried on by [ongoing religious affections] to the end of life; till it is brought to perfection in glory. Hence the progress of the work of grace in the hearts of the saints, is represented in Scripture as a continued conversion and renovation of nature.[10]

To draw on the figures we discussed in our first chapter, the picture we get of conversion and nurture in Edwards is more like the story of Dorothy Day than like that of Augustine. One senses in Augustine that the affections were being shaped prior to conversion. Conversion affirmed and confirmed all that had gone before. With Dorothy Day the conversion and baptism were like that little seed, a slight incursion of the light, and through Peter Maurin and the Catholic Worker Movement she grew in—grew into—grace.

What we owe Edwards in relation to our concerns for commitment and nurture, is first of all respect for his assumption that true conversion bore true fruit and that one could raise questions about the efficacy of even the most sublime religious experience.

And what we owe him, second, is the reminder, as John E. Smith says of him, that

the motivation of the revivalist in every period is a vivid sense of the personal character of religious faith. He sees that conventionalism is the death of religion, and that each individual must confront the issues and make the decision for himself; there is no faith by proxy.[11]

Here is precisely where Horace Bushnell would provide a caveat, and perhaps a corrective. While there is no doubt that

Bushnell believed in the personal nature of religious faith, he believed equally strongly in its organic qualities. Faith was imparted as well as decided. It was nurtured at home and church as well as implanted by God, or it was implanted by God through the nurture of home and church.

Bushnell himself was converted at a Yale revival in 1831, and he often preached the need for commitment and decision, but he came to an even deeper experience of God through the tragedy of the death of his child. Furthermore, he spent his ministry in competition with another Congregational minister in Hartford who was famous for his revivals. Perhaps this helped spark some of Bushnell's distrust:

> The only difficulty I have ever encountered in my ministry, that cost me a real and deep trial of feeling, related to the matter of evangelist preachers, and what may be called the machinery system of revivals. Things had come to such a pitch in the churches, by the intensity of the revival system, that the permanent was sacrificed to the casual, the ordinary swallowed up and lost in the extraordinary, and Christian piety itself reduced to a kind of campaigning or stage-effect exercise.[12]

The first version of Bushnell's *Discourses on Christian Nurture* was published in 1847, one century and one year after Edwards' *Treatise Concerning Religious Affections*, and the second, fuller version was published in 1861.

The heart of Bushnell's concern is clear when he writes about "the ostrich nurture," parents who, ostrich-like, leave their offspring to fend for themselves. Some mistaken people:

> make a merit of great persistency and firmness, in asserting the universal necessity of a new spiritual birth; not perceiving under what varieties of form that change may be wrought. The soul must be exercised, they think, in one given way, viz.: by a struggle with sin, a conscious self-renunciation, and a true turning to Christ for mercy, followed by the joy and peace of a new life in the Spirit. A child, in other words, can be born of God only in the same way that an adult can.[13]

Bushnell's answer to this mistaken single-mindedness lies in his affirmation of the organic aspects of faith—the essential role of human community, especially the family, but also the church, in nurturing the child toward faith. Thus Bushnell provides a strong defense of family prayers, infant baptism, children admitted to the communion table. (Edwards got in trouble in part by trying to be very strict about who took communion.)

Bushnell responds to Edwards directly:

> the Great Revival, under Whitfield and Edwards, inaugurated and brought up to its highest intensity the new era of individualism—the same overwrought, misapplied scheme of personal experience in religion, which has continued with some modifications to the present day. . . . [This religion] makes nothing of the family, and the church, and the organic powers God has constituted as vehicles of grace.[14]

Bushnell understandably loves 2 Timothy 3:14: "But as for you, continue in what you have learned and firmly believed, knowing from whom you have learned it." Bushnell is sure that the "from whom" is Timothy's mother, a paradigm of Christian nurture. "But I must speak, in closing," writes Bushnell,

> of what appears to be a somewhat general misconception, as respects *the aim* of Christian teaching in the case of very young children. According to the view I am here maintaining, it is not their conversion, in the sense commonly given to that term. That is a notion which belongs to the scheme that makes nothing of baptism and the organic unity of the house; that looks upon the children as being heathens, or aliens, requiring, of course, to be converted. But according to the scheme here presented, they are not heathens, or aliens; but they are in and of the household of faith, and their growing up is to be in the same. Parents, therefore, in the religious teaching of their children, are not to have it as a point of fidelity to press them into some crisis of high experience, called conversion. Their teaching is to be that which feeds a growth, not that which stirs a revolution. It is to be nurture, presuming on a grace already and always given.[15]

We need to place Bushnell in relationship to other figures in our discussion. To an extent, Monica, Auguatine's mother, fits Bushnell's model of the nurturing parent, though what she wrought through her prayers was an odd combination of growth and revolution. Perhaps the story of Augustine suggests that Bushnell, against his own better principles, sometimes decides that within the household of faith there is only one way.

Unlike Paul, and with the pastorals, Bushnell clearly seems himself in a time and situation where institutions—church, school, state—are going to be around for a long while and where faith can use and profit from such institutions.

There is much in Bushnell to applaud and appreciate. What I said about my own history, in the first chapter of this essay, indicates how Bushnellian was my own upbringing, and I think one could trace a line from Bushnell to much of the American Protestant liberalism that was my own theological background. Among the charms and strengths of Bushnell, furthermore, is his strong affirmation of children and their worth and his telling insights into who they are, what touches them. His theological and psychological acumen come together when Bushnell suggests that children should be encouraged in their play, because the play of children embodies and foreshadows the gift of Christian liberty.[16]

Finally, in other modes and circumstances Bushnell sounds far more evangelical. In *Christian Nurture* he clearly is fighting a battle against a particular revivalistic mode of child evangelism. When he himself mounts the pulpit, the call for decision can be clear:

> This is the salvation that our God is working in his Son, but as the great apostle here intimates, it is, and is to be, by faith; for the result can never be issued save as we, on our part believe. . . . And this we do in faith. Faith is the act by which one being confides in another. . . . For it is even your chance of salvation, as a lost man, that a being has come into the world, so great in character and feeling, that turning to be with him, he shall be with you.[17]

And preaching on the text that led to Augustine's conversion, Bushnell said:

How then do we put [Christ] on? By faith, I answer, only by faith. For in that the soul comes to him, shivering in the cold shame of its sin, and gives itself over to him, to be loved, protected, covered in, by his gracious life and passion. . . . Your iniquities are thus to be forgiven, your sin to be covered.[18]

What does this brief and selective historical survey suggest about evangelism, Christian education, and the world in which both take place?

In Paul, Edwards, and Bushnell, evangelism and education combine. In Paul the combination is a remarkable tension or synthesis. In Edwards and Bushnell there is special weight given to the one side or the other.

Our study of these representative figures may help us place ourselves historically. Do we trust the processes of history and the institutions of family, (state), and church—along with the pastorals and Horace Bushnell? Or do we see this as a time of crisis, of the shaking of the foundations—with Paul and Jonathan Edwards? Perhaps the assumptions of Horace Bushnell were more appropriate to American Christendom than to this post-Christian era when we can hardly count on much nurture at home, or perhaps even in the church.

What does seem clear is that nurture which never leads to decision can nurture vague Judaeo-Christian values but not much Christian conviction. What does seem clear is that evangelism which does not move on to nurture can produce the vivid but shallow faith that Edwards feared, or produce Chrstianity like that of the Corinthians—full of the Spirit but without much sense of responsibility for the world around them.

We also live with a concern which for various reasons touched Paul, the pastorals, Edwards, and Bushnell less than it touches us: How do both evangelism and nurture move beyond one's sense of salvation and love for the neighbor to a commitment to economic and social justice and to reconciliation in a broken world?

The Journey Ahead: Possibilities and Hope

by David L. Bartlett

Our first two chapters dealt with the past, though it was of course a selected past, a usable past. Augustine, Dorothy Day, St. Paul, the pastoral epistles, Jonathan Edwards, Horace Bushnell are paradigmatic figures because their stories still illumine our stories. Where they correct excesses, they correct our own excesses. When they bring insight they enlighten our own situation as well as theirs.

In this chapter I want to begin by a brief analysis of the current dichotomy between nurture and conversion, and then I want to look at some signs of hope in statements emerging from people in the mainline ecumenical movement. Then I want to make three proposals as a guide to the future. I will present them briefly and return to them at the end.

I will test the proposals by a more empirical study, though not a scientific one, a study of three quite different churches in the East Bay area of Northern California.

Then I will return to the three principles and flesh them out.

I.

E. Stanley Jones, writing several decades ago, nonetheless puts our current hope and dilemma in perspective from his own standpoint:

> At the end of every bit of knowledge in any realm is a moral choice—what will I do with that knowledge? The knowledge itself is not healing—the moral choice is.

It is pre-eminently true in religious education. The knowledge about the Scriptures, about God, about Christ, about the moral laws is not in itself healing. At the end of this knowledge is a choice . . . .

Religious education should lead inevitably to a moral and spiritual choice—it should lead inevitably to conversion. But has it? Very often it has been substituted for conversion. The consequence is that the churches are filled with unconverted people. They know about God, but they don't know Him.[1]

On the other side, Garland Knott in a paper directed to our concerns, reminds those whose special stress is on evangelism, that they cannot ignore what Christian education brings to the process of conversion:

Finally, evangelists cannot ignore education as a primary source of Christian converts. On occasion it may be that a lifelong blasphemer, drunkard, and lecher will undergo a spectacular conversion; and all are thankful when that happens. However, the great majority of those who as adolescents or young adults profess faith in Christ have experienced years of preparation in the Sunday school or other educational programs.[2]

Furthermore, as Jonathan Edwards' writings continue to remind us, when it comes to conversion all that glistens is not gold. Not every apparent conversion results in new life, and often what seems to help in the nurture of new life ia precisely *nurture*: those educational, pastoral, and catechetical programs and processes which bring the implanted seed of grace to fruition.

Relatively recent statements from ecumenical bodies suggest that a movement toward conversation between those whose emphasis is evangelism and those whose emphasis is education is underway.

The 1976 Policy Statement, *Evangelism Today*, adopted by the Governing Board of the National Council of Churches, points to the way in which evangelism moves toward community, includes ongoing nurture, and issues in practical movements toward justice:

The commitment to Jesus Christ is a profound event. It is a *personal* event; by the power of the Holy Spirit sinners experience the divine forgiveness and commit themselves to live obediently to Christ the living Lord. It is a *social* event; relationships with friends, neighbors and family are radically altered by the revolutionary demands and allowances of divine love. It is a *community* event; it engrafts one into the community of believers, the church. It is a *public* event; new confrontations with the institutions of society occur, for the "principalities and power" which impoverish and enslave humanity cannot go unchallenged by Christians! . . .

The task of evangelism today is calling people to repentance, to faith in Jesus Christ, to study God's word, to continue steadfast in prayer, and to bearing witness to Him.[3]

The Cooperative Curriculum Project of 1965 stated the objective of the curriculum:

The objective of Christian education is that all persons be aware of God, through his self-disclosure, especially his redeeming love as revealed in Jesus Christ, and that they respond in faith and love—to the end that they may know who they are and what the human situation means, grow as sons [and daughters] of God rooted in the Christian community, live in the Spirit of God in every relationship, fulfill their common discipleship in the world, and abide in the Christian hope.[4]

What is clear in both the curriculum objective and the Policy Statement is the sense, as E. Stanley Jones would affirm, that Christian education is not just knowing about God but knowing God, not just understanding Jesus but following him as obedient disciples. What is missing in the curriculum statement is perhaps sufficient attention to the role of choice and decision in the matter of faith. God's self-disclosure seems to occur *through* the curriculum without sufficient attention to the question: How do you respond? Do you believe? Do you repent and trust in the gospel?

The Mission and Evangelism Statement approved by the Central Committee of the World Council of Churches in July,

1982, insists that evangelism, and I would add nurture, does not exist alone for the sake of the believer nor for the sake of the church but for the sake of God's justice in the world:

> Conversion happens in the midst of our historical reality and incorporates the totality of our life, because God's love is concerned with that totality. Jesus' call is an invitation to follow him joyfully, to participate in his servant body, to share with him in the struggle to overcome sin, poverty and death.
>
> There is no evangelism without solidarity; there is no Christian solidarity that does not involve sharing the knowledge of the kingdom which is God's promise to the poor of the earth.[5]

These ecumenical statements help point to three premises that I propose as guidelines on the quest for a richer bonding between commitment and nurture—as signs of hope for the future. None is strikingly or even mildly original, but these premises represent (I hope) the best of our shared hope and the best of what we have learned from our forebears like Paul, Edwards, Bushnell, Augustine, and Dorothy Day.

My attempt is to look at both evangelism and nurture from the larger perspective of *discipleship*, I simply state my premises now, then will test them out empirically and return finally for elaboration.

1. Christian education which nurtures discipleship will not only deepen understanding, it will call for commitment.

2. Evangelism which calls for discipleship will not only seek commitment, it will encourage growth in understanding and deepening of the Christian gifts of faith, hope, and love. (A corollary to this is that evangelism which calls for discipleship will acknowledge the ways in which families, society, and the church can provide preparation for the gospel—as understanding is nascent, and faith, hope, and love are nurtured even prior to the crisis of commitment.)

3. The disciple lives not for the sake of the self, nor for the sake of the church, but for the sake of Christ in the world. In our time, and by the light given to us, that means a particular attention to the poor and oppressed of the world, but of course it does not only mean that.

74

II.

With these premises in mind I wanted to see what was actually going on in three churches. They were chosen in part because I knew about them and knew that their clergy were self-conscious about the offices of ministry and observant about what was going on in their own congregations. The churches were also sufficiently distinct from one another that different senses of the problems and hopes of local congregations would likely emerge from our converaations.

The first congregation studied was St. Mark's Church in Berkeley, an Episcopal church where Philip Getchell is the rector. I chose this church in part because of friends who were parishioners who admired the congregation and Getchell's leadership. I chose the church in part because of the influence on contemporary social analysis of the book by Robert Bellah and others, *Habits of the Heart*.[7] In that book St. Mark's appears as St. Stephen's, and Father Getchell appears as Father Morrison. *Habits of the Heart* shows the ways in which that church combines worship, especially the eucharist, with social action, So I wanted to talk with Father Getchell about how St. Mark's combined evangelism and Christian education.

Two words about the following report. As with all three of my "case studies," it is based entirely on the insights of the congregation's clerical leadership and is therefore clearly unscientific and subjective. And, as with the other studies, the material is organized only in terms of themes and concerns which interested the interviewer—subjectivity multiplied.

St. Mark's is a church of about 500 members, largely but not exclusively middle class, predominantly white, in a neighborhood near the University of California. In the community, business and professional people live fairly near at hand and Berkeley street people are very much in evidence. As with other city churches, you need to go through a security system to get into the building.

Father Getchell and I talked first about evangelism, though issues related to nurture quickly emerged. Evangelism at St. Mark's can be contrasted to the approach of a large church down the street that is closely tied to Inter-Varsity and that includes as part of its regular appeal the need to make a decision, now, for Jesus, and the call to "come out" of the world.

Theologically, says Getchell, Anglicans stress the continuity between nature and grace, between faith and reason. In his preaching and his teaching he not only uses the lectionary but seeks to give reasoned arguments for the faith, trusting the Holy Spirit to illumine not only the heart but the mind. (In this combination Getchell sounds very Edwardsian.) This relates to his concern to provide psychological space for those who come to visit at St. Mark's, to let them worship without feeling any pressure for immediate decision. Given time and space and friendly persuasion, many do decide to become part of the church. Some of these have been members of Episcopal churches elsewhere, some come from other denominations, some come from no church background at all.

Those who have not been previously churched undergo an intensive program of care and catechesis through the months leading up to their confirmation or baptism. Each person is assigned an individual shepherd, and that shepherd helps lead the new member toward decision-making, a decision that is now informed both by study and by the care of a church member. When a new member is received, he or she repeats vows that establish the way in which commitment will lead to discipleship.

There is the promise to follow Jesus Christ, to break bread in the eucharist and share in prayers, to live at peace with one's neighbors, and to work for peace and justice in the world.

Both leading up to and growing out of this process of shepherding and evangelism, the church has the whole range of church education activities for both children and adults.

The curriculum used for children is a mixture of denominational, ecumenical, and homegrown material. Those who structure curriculum at St. Mark's are working toward the as yet unconsummated goal of focusing on the lectionary in such a way that in any given week the whole life of the church moves out of the same scriptural center.

Adult education consists of a mix of Bible study and more culturally related classes, arts festivals, and study groups on issues.

Through a group of pastors studying the lectionary together each Tuesday morning, St. Mark's, like other East Bay churches, became part of the East Bay Sanctuary covenant and continues strong and active in that movement. The study group provides a stunning example of Bible study leading to concrete action for justice.

My sense is that the classes of the church provide nurture for those who are already committed, and for some also provide an entree as they begin to think about the possibility of Christian commitment.

Why do people come to St. Mark's, and why do they join? There are a variety of reasons. Some come for the preaching, some for the worship, some for the music, some seeking friends, some wanting a way to work in the community, or for justice on a larger scale. A few take a course in Milton or Plato at the university and want to make connections.

Finally, Father Getchell's sense is that when people join St. Mark's they are somewhere different theologically and perhaps even chronologically than when they join the larger church down the street. They are older and more questioning; there are fewer freshmen and more graduate students.

What signs of hope emerge from our study of St. Mark's? It is clearly a church that takes both education and evangelism with great seriousness, where the assumption is that faith will seek understanding and that sometimes understanding will seek faith.

It is a church that insists that faith issue in discipleship, though not without dissent and tension sometimes over the shape that discipleship will take.

What would have been helpfully made more clear? The Baptist interviewer, at least, might have looked for more attention to the relationship between education and evangelism in preaching. And in terms of the theme of this book we might have looked for a clearer sense of how the church school relates both to the social ministry and to the outreach of the church.

*

The second church we studied is the McGee Avenue Baptist Church, also in Berkeley. McGee Avenue's membership is almost entirely black. The church has about 800 members, 600 of them active. The Rev. James Stewart has been the pastor for the past fifteen years.

Pastor Stewart had clearly given considerable time to thinking about the relationship between evangelism and education in his ministry and his congregation. "My basic premise," he said, "is that evangelism and Christian education are inseparable. They're inseparable in theory and they are inseparable in the practice of the church."

According to Stewart the center of the church's life is worship, and the center of worship is preaching. James Stewart sees his preaching as being primarily educational. His sermons are issue-oriented, but at the same time he hopes that he always carries an evangelical thrust, seeking to proclaim the gospel to those who need to make their commitment. Interestingly, in terms of evangelism and nurture, Stewart also sees preaching as group counseling. He has just finished advanced work in pastoral care at Holy Names College. He is doing more and more pastoral counseling in his ministry, and he sees the sermon as a means of dealing with the problems of a whole group of people at the same time.

The church's motto, drawn from the national concerns of the American Baptist denomination is "Grow by Caring." To this motto they add the scriptural injunction: "Hold fast the word of God." McGee Avenue's diaconate are trained to have watch care over groups of members, both as a matter of outreach and as a means of maintenance, though this way of structuring care has not been uniformly successful.

The church school is definitely seen as a means of evangelism. Each new youth who moves into the neighborhood is assigned a sponsor, not just to show him or her around the church, but to show the newcomer around the neighborhood and the school. Youth ministry has a strong component of Bible study, and part of the purpose of the study is to lead young people to a decision for Christ. Indeed, the church school throughout, from infants to adults, has an evangelistic thrust. The purpose, says Stewart, is not only education but education moving toward decision.

The one additional full-time staff member is the minister of Christian education.

Not only is education a means of evangelism, but when folk decide to join the church they enter into a process of education and deepening discipline. Each new member is required to attend four classes taught by the pastor: (1) What is it to be a Christian? (2) What is it to be a church member? (3) What is it to be a Baptist? (4)What is it to be part of a covenant community, with special stress on the church covenant of McGee Avenue Baptist Church.

Nonetheless, despite these structures of caring and instruction, Pastor Stewart says there is the continual problem of losing people out the back door. They make a decision for membership, come for a while, and then over time simply drift away.

In summarizing the thrust of his own ministry, Stewart says that his goal above all has been to reverse the inward trend of McGee's ministry and to move the folk outward toward the community and the world. Locally, the church has a hot food program, a food pantry, a clothing closet and a senior center, which has recently outgrown the church facility. Internationally, the church twice took money from their building fund to provide famine relief for people in Africa, postponing Stewart's dream of presiding over the dedication of a greatly expanded building, but the impetus for this mission giving has come largely from him.

Pastor Stewart also admits that he has by no means the unanimous support of the congregation in this stress on community action and world service, but he feels that on the whole he has been able to bring the congregation along with him. He further admits that when his church members talk about his accomplishments, they are less apt to notice the outward thrust and more apt to commend him on making good deals on real estate for the church's future expansion.

There is much to praise and commend in the ministry of McGee Avenue Church. There is a self-conscious connection between evangelism and nurture and an expanding commitment to the relationship between personal faith ahd social concerns. There is a ministry which is both deeply Baptist and avowedly ecumenical.

What more might one have hoped for? Some further solutions to the problem of attrition, and some sense of how the diaconate in their care-giving might be inspired and enabled to watch more adequately after their flocks. (I state the problem in part because the church I know best shares it.) And perhaps one might have hoped for some clearer sense of how the church's mission could include fighting against the principalities and powers that lead to economic injustice as well as providing relief to those in need.

*

The third church on which I reflected is the Lakeshore Avenue Baptist Church, across the city line in Oakland, California. The church has a membership of about four hundred, and the membership is almost equally divided between black and white people in a situation that is remarkably stable. That is, new members who join are also drawn equally from the black and white communities. There is a very modest hispanic presence and a more significant Asian-American membership. Like St, Mark's, the church is also known to include in its membership a small but significant minority of gay men and lesbian women. The church is predominantly, almost exclusively, middle middle class. I am pastor of the church, now in my sixth year there.

Historically, the church's great sense of its mission rested on its radio ministry. Until two years ago it sponsored the "oldest continuous daily religious broadcast" in America, a program sixty years old when it was reluctantly discontinued. So strongly was the church's sense of self linked with this radio ministry that, when the congregation's latest meeting house was built in 1957, considerably greater attention was paid to adequate equipment and acoustics for broadcasting than was paid to adequate space for Christian education or even for church socializing.

The radio ministry in its early years drew considerable numbers of people to the church, especially for the Sunday night service where the pastor took on the issues of the day, with a strong bias toward the social gospel.

Under my predecessor, who has a strong mystical bent, a number of radio visitors came regularly to the Sunday service, but very few of these joined, and when the Lord called him to serve in Seattle, that crew largely disappeared.

More than being a means of evangelism, the radio ministry provided a mixture of education and pastoral care—our own version of what James Stewart does in his preaching. The surveys told us that thousands of people listened to the church's program on their way to work or over the breakfast table each morning. Our hope is that some of these were strengthened in their commitments to faith and to their own churches. Only a handful in recent years joined our church as a result of this outreach ministry. Furthermore, unlike our earliest years, in recent years we were heard on an all-religious station, so we did not much reach the unchurched or the irreligious.

The daily radio program died when new station management fired us from our accustomed slot in order to make the theological tone of morning prime time more to their liking. In some ways the church has been trying to find out what to do about evangelism, mission, and perhaps even Christian education since. While for many churches media ministry is the new wave, for us it was the venerable tradition, and we look and wait for some contemporary means of outreach and service.

Certainly as of now the most visible and probably the most successful means of outreach is the morning worship service. In that service, whatever the results, everyone works hard to provide worship which glorifies God, as Jonathan Edwards would insist, but which also attracts worshipers. The preaching is from the lectionary, and for that and other reasons tends to run the gamut of theological focuses and homiletical purposes. Evangelism is kept self-consciously as part of what we are about.

As with James Stewart, I know that most of our folk will get their only biblical and theological education in any given week from the worship service, and the teaching function of preaching is important to us. Related to this, sermons are preceded, ten days before, by evening sermon seminars where church members gather to hear the preacher's exegetical thoughts and join together in seeking clues to the application of the texts to our common life, a practice I borrowed from East Harlem Protestant Parish.

On the other hand, education is a growing part of our ministry, with membership in church school for children just about doubling in the past three years (from about 35 to about 70). This growth is partly the result of careful attention to stronger Christian education and partly a result of our social concern. We have sponsored several refugee families who have become a part of the congregation, bringing their large and lively families into our church school program. For others, there is no doubt that church school provides their entree into the community of faith—sometimes children who come without their parents, sometimes children who come and later bring their parents, or at least as often, their parent.

We provide membership classes for new and potential members, but more sporadically and less thoroughly than either St. Mark's or McGee Avenue. Each new church member has a sponsor, but there is nothing like the careful spiritual shepherding that St. Mark's provides through their sponsorship program.

Like McGee Avenue we are divided into about thirty shep-

81

herding goups, with shepherds assigned to watch over their flocks by night ad day, keeping touch and reporting any problems or special needs. As with McGee, we find that about half of those shepherding groups are functioning very well.

Despite, or because of these well-intentioned but somewhat ill-formed programs, our greatest danger is that many will come to our worship, join our church, never do anything more than attend the worship, and because they lack both sufficient nurture and sufficient community, quietly drift away.

Our church's belief, often stated and sometimes acted out, is that commitment to the church is also commitment to Christ's work in and for the world. Our Hunger Task Force has been going strong for years, growing out of an adult education class, and now including educational, fund-raising, and service components. Our Central America Affinity Group studies and prays and may one day find a way to enter the East Bay Sanctuary Covenant without dragging the rest of the congregation along—a congregation not eager to be dragged. Our hope for our pending stewardship campaign is to stress our life as a covenant community and to ask each member to covenant to one particular service in the church and one particular service in the community.

Our greatest pride is in our diversity and inclusiveness. That is belied somewhat by the fact that blacks have held every position of leadership in our congregation—save ordained clergyperson. And our inclusiveness is tested by the presence of gay men and lesbian women among us. For some that continues to be a stumbling block. For others it is part of our attraction; in particular for church folk who are not themselves gay or lesbian but who have children or brothers or sisters who are, find among us a place to be honest about their own families and their own concerns.

What more would I hope? An adult educational program which included more than one tenth of the adult membership of the church and was intentional in its planning toward discipleship. A non-white pastor on the staff. More Hispanic presence in the congregation. Shepherding that more consistently shepherded. A sense of commitment to membership which included some deeper sense of responsibility for all members. Patience on the part of all.

III.

So, finally, what do I see for the future in terms of the ministry of evangelism and the ministry of Christian education? I present my hopes, and what I see in the churches I visit and in the interests of the larger church suggest that these hopes are neither foolish nor fruitless.

I return to my three premises.

1. *Christian education that nurtures discipleship will not only deepen understanding, it will ask commitment.*

It may be part of the gift of the black church, certainly it is a gift of McGee Avenue Church, that it unashamedly assumes that education moves toward commitment. As a Baptist, some of whose family has preached and worshiped in the Hartford Baptist churches that Bushenll berated for their stress on evangelism, I couldn't help thinking that he underestimated what believers' baptism can mean in the universal church. Surely the insistence on a moment of commitment, a public declaration of one's faith, is not inconsistent with an understanding that many of us are nurtured toward faith through family, community, friends.

Augustine would not have got to read St. Paul in the garden had Monica not been nurturing and nagging him, but it took St. Paul in the garden to get Augustine to commit himself to the faith for which Monica had been praying.

My sense in the churches I visited and the conversations I have with concerned church people is that few would be so totally committed to spiritual evolution as to deny the essential need for saying: Here I stand.

2. *Evangelism that calls for discipleship will not only seek commitment, it will encourage growth in understanding, and a deepening of the Christian gifts of faith, hope, and love.*

None of the three churches I studied thinks that when a decision is made to become a Christian or to join that congregation, the important work is over. Each knows that through preaching, worship, church school, study groups, and sponsorship the discipline of discipleship goes on and on.

Related to this is a claim picked up from my years at the University of Chicago. We need to honor the orders of creation as well as the orders of redemption. That is to say that evangelists may not always want to convince by talking of bondage to sin but may sometimes convince by pointing to intimations of grace and hints of providence—the gifts not only of nurturing parents or a nurturing community but of a nurturing and providential God. Augustine's *Confessions* are not just the statement that at the end God bailed him out, but the grateful acknowledgement that it was God who led him all the way.

3. *The disciple (the converted and being-educated Christian) lives not for the sake of the self, nor for the sake of the church, but for the sake of Christ in the world.* In our time and by the light that is given to us, that means a particular attention to the poor and oppressed of the world, but of course it does not mean only that.

We should all be very nervous about Christian education that leads to budding young theologians, long on knowledge but short on compassion toward the oppressed. We should all be exceedingly nervous about any evangelism movements which suggest that, if we get people pouring into the churches as in the 50s, we will have done God's work and our own and can say, as we fill our granaries with these newly converted sheaves, "Now, my soul, take thy rest." The power of the gospel is never measured by the size of our congregations, and the mission of the church is never primarily self-aggrandizement. Evangelism and discipleship go hand in hand.

What I find most promising in the three churches I studied and in scores and scores of others, is that all of them see themselves as seeking not only to turn inward but to turn outward to the world. They believe, with Dorothy Day, that when we are catechized and baptized, we've only just begun.

Notes

Reading #1 Faith Journeys
1. Augustine, *The Confessions*, trans. John K. Ryan. Doubleday, 1960. Book VIII, Chapter 7, 17.
2. *Confessions*, VIII, 8, 19. And see Peter Brown, *Augustine of Hippo: A Biography*. University of California Press, 1967, p. 107.
3. *Confessions*, VIII, 8, 28-29.
4. Brown, *ibid.*, p. 124.
5. *Confessions*, I, 11, 17.
6. *Ibid.*, III, 11, 19.
7. *Ibid.*, VIII, 12, 30.
8. *Ibid.*, I, 11, 17.
9. *Ibid.*, III, 4, 7-8. See also Brown, *Ibid.*, p. 40.
10. *Confessions*, VII, 10, 16.
11. *Ibid.*, V, 14, 23.
12. *Ibid.*, IV, 4, 9.
13. *Ibid.*, VI, 15, 25.
14. *Ibid.*, IV, 9, 14.
15. *Ibid.*, II, 4, 9.
16. See *Confessions*, IX, 2, 4, and Brown, *Ibid.*, pp. 109-110.
17. Dorothy Day, *The Long Loneliness*. Harper & Row, 1952, p. 159.
18. *Ibid.*, p. 155.
19. *Ibid.*, pp. 169-170.
20. *Ibid.*, p. 10.
21. *Ibid.*, pp. 19-20.
22. *Ibid.*, p. 26.
23. See William D. Miller, *Dorothy Day: A Biography*. Harper & Row, 1982, for a fuller account of these years.
24. Miller, *ibid.*, pp. 198-199.
25. Day, *Loneliness*, p. 163.
26. *Ibid.*, p. 9.
27. Dorothy Day, *Loaves and Fishes*. Harper & Row, 1963,p. 26.

Reading #2 The Journey in our History
1. See David L. Bartlett, *Paul's Vision for the Teaching Church*. Judson Press, 1977.
2. For this insight into the theology of the pastorals I am indebted to Lewis R. Donelson, *Pseudepigraphy and Ethical Argument in the Pastoral Epistles*. Tubingen: J. C. B. Mohr/ Paul Siebeck, 1986, pp. 115-191.
3. In Clarence H. Faust and Thomas H. Johnson, eds., *Jonathan Edwards: Representative Selections*. New York: Hill and Wang, 1962, p. 196.

4. Jonathan Edwards, *A Treatise Concerning Religious Affections*, ed. by John E. Smith, in *Works of Jonathan Edwards* (Volume II). Yale University Press, 1959, p. 275.

5. Sydney Ahlstrom, *A Religious History of the Amnerican People*. Yale University Press, 1972, p. 298.

6. *Ibid.*, p. 299.

7. Edwards, *ibid.*, p. 266.

8. *Ibid.*, p. 382, cf. p. 390.

9. *Ibid.*, pp. 344-345.

10. *Ibid.*, p. 343.

11. In the introduction to Edwards, *ibid.*, p. 49.

12. Horace Bushnell, "Twentieth Anniversary: A Commemorative Discourse Delivered in the North Church of Hartford, May 22, 1853./ Quoted by John Mulder in the introduction to Bushnell's *Christian Nurture. Grand Rapids; Baker Book House, 1909, p. xix.

13. *Ibid.*, p. 73.

14. *Ibid.*, p. 187.

15. *Ibid.*, p. 381.

16. *Ibid.*, pp. 339-340.

17. In Horace Bushnell, *Sermons on Christ and His Salvation*. Charles Scribner's Sons, 1901, pp. 90-91. (First published in 1864.)

18. *Ibid.*, pp. 424-425.

Reading #3 The Journey Ahead: Possibilities and Hope

1. E. Stanley Jones, *Conversion*. Abingdon Press, 1959, p. 180.

2. Garland Knott, "Evangelism and Christian Education: Partners in Ministry." Division of Education and Ministry: National Council of Churches of Christ in the U.S.A., c. 1986, p. 11.

3. "Evangelism Today: A Policy Statement of the National Council of the Churches of Christ in the United States of America," Adopted by the Governing Board, March 3, 1976. 37.1-2

4. From *The Church's Educational Ministry: A Curriculum Plan*. Bethany Press, 1966, p. 8.

5. "Mission and Evangelism—An Ecumenical Affirmation." Approved by the Central Committee, World Council of Churches, July, 1982. Published in *International Review of Mission*, Vol. LXXI, No. 284 (October, 1984), pp. 433, 441..

6. Robert N. Bellah, Richard Madsen, William M. Sullivan, Ann Swidler, and Steven M. Tipton, *Habits of the Heart*. University of California Press, 1985. See especially pp. 239- 243.

Selected Bibliography

Storyweaving: Using Stories to Transform Your Congregation, a book by Peter M. Morgan. Order from Christian Board of Publication, Box 179, St. Louis, MO 63166.

Vision for Mission Resources, a leaflet published by The American Lutheran Church, 422 South Fifth Street, Minneapolis, MN 55415.

Witness Curriculum, a curriculum series, published by Augsburg Publishing House, 422 South Fifth Street, Minneapolis, MN 55415.

Youth: Reach Them, Keep Them, a leaflet by Cheryl Reames and Crystal Zinkiewicz, 1986. Graded Press of the United Methodist Publishing House. Available from Cokesbury.

The Relationship Between Evangelism and Catechesis, a study paper by Rev. Robert J. Hater, 1981. National Conferennce of Diocesan Directors of Religious Education, 1312 Massachusetts Avenue NW, Washington, DC 20005.

Teaching for Commitment, a leaflet by Ruth McDowell, 1986. Graded Press of the United Methodist Publishing House. Available from Cokesbury.

People of the Covenant, a program of the Church of the Brethren General Board, 1451 Dundee Avenue, Elgin, IL 60120.

The Catechumenate: A Curriculum Model (A Place for Evangelism to Root Itself). Rev. Wayne Schwap, Coordinator, Evangelism Ministry, The Episcopal Church, 815 Second Avenue, New York, NY 10017.

For additional resources and ideas you may write:

National Council of Church of Christ
Commission on Worship and Evangelism
473 Riverside Drive, 5th Floor
New York, NY 10115

Division of Education and Ministry
475 Riverside Drive, 7th Floor
New York, NY 10115

World Council of Churches
Programme Unit Ii, Education and Renewal
150 Route de Ferney
1211 Geneva 20, Switzerland

Additional Readings

Evangelism and Christian Education
Partners in Ministry

(The following are from a paper by this title by Garland Knott, Professor of Religion, Methodist College, Copyright 1986, Division of Education and Ministry, National Council of Churches of Christ in the U.S.A.)

There has been a long history of opposition between advocates of evangelism and advocates of Christian education in North American churches. This struggle dates back to the old wars between fundamentalism and liberalism in the Protestant communions and between traditionalism and modernism among Roman Catholics. . . .

In a number of denominations around the country there is an uneasy truce between evangelism and Christian education. There is much lip-service to the ideas of mutual respect and cooperation, but one has to spend only a little while with persons in leadership positions to recognize that difficulties and even animosities still linger. . . .

What specific matters are at issue? What do they believe about each other that gives them pause? (Keep in mind that there are always individual exceptions.)

Evangelistically-minded Christians generally believe that nineteenth century liberal theology is still the leading spirit in religious education today. No doubt North American religious education grew up with liberalism, and its professional leadership was dominated by such a view during the first forty years of the twentieth century. (This is *theological* liberalism, which has no necessary connection with political liberalism.) . . .

Consequently, denominational curriculum plans may be viewed by some as inadequate because they spend large blocks of time on topics other than sin and salvation. and because secular discoveries about human development and the human life cycle form an important part of their foundation. If there is to be Christian education, it ought to be Bible study, always and everywhere.

88

Religious educators, on the other hand, may accuse evangelists of denying our full humanity. Reason, they say, is just as much a gift of God as faith, and it ought to be used. In fact, knowledge is a necessary basis for faith. Educators tend to think of evangelists as persons who glory in ignorance and reduce faith to assent grounded purely in emotionalism.

More tellingly yet, educators frequently say that evangelistic types are reluctant to examine their faith for fear that it may not stand the test of reason. In this way a statement of deep commitment is construed as an attempt to deny insecurity and self-doubt. . . .

What Say the Scriptures?

It is extremely valuable to know that both of the ministries under discussion find ample warrant in the Bible. This is true of the Old Testament as well as the New. In the next two sections there will be an examination of this grounding in Scripture. It is possible here to do this only in rather broad terms, leaving the location of specific passages largely to the reader who wishes to pursue the matter further.

Foundations of evangelism are found in the Old Testament in the unmerited love of God shown to Israel. The people are chosen not because of any inherent goodness (the contrary can be shown), but simply because God loves them and has promised to save them. Here is the doctrine of grace which lies at the heart of evangelism.

The prophets warned that God would punish the sins of Israel, but in the preaching of Hosea God's redemptive purpose for this was revealed. Later prophets foretold the restoration of Israel and with it the accession of all nations to the glorious message of God. When Jesus read the scripture in a synagogue near his home, he chose a passage from Isaiah 61 whose whole spirit is that of proclaiming the good news. The Old Testament is part of Christian scripture, and it is a rich source for evangelism.

It is equally true to say that Christian education has profound origins in the life and writings of the Hebrew people. The best English translation of the word *torah* is probably "teaching." The priests were responsible for Torah, and one of their most prominent duties was to teach the tradition to their sons who would succeed them, and to all others who wished it. It was the priests who preserved the scripture during the Exile and established the foundations of Judaism.

However, the responsibility for teaching extended far beyond the priesthood to all Israel. This truth is made obvious by a reading of the passage known as the Shema, found in Deuteronomy 6:4-9. Israel is to understand that there is only one God, who is to be loved with all the heart, soul, and might. Moreover, the people are to teach the words of

God diligently to their children. Thus did Israel become a teaching/learning community, laying the foundation for the church in later times.

Old Testament prophecy concerns itself with two ways of knowing God. One of these is the knowledge of God's will and commandments—what God is like. The other is through close association with and commitment to God as a Person, as Friend and Redeemer. Both of these ways are vital. Thus in one tradition there is the unification of primary concerns for both education and evangelism.

The four gospels are each in its own way a proclamation of the good news about Jesus and the kingdom. Their purpose is to engender belief in the depths of the reader's being. They call for a decision to be made. The very word "evangelism" comes from the Greek word *evangelion*, which we translate as "gospel."

Likewise the gospels are instruments of Christian teaching. They are the only substantive accounts of what Jesus said and did. Part of the reason for the gospels is instructional, "that you may know the truth concerning the things of which you have been informed" (Luke 1:4). The Gospel of Matthew seems likely to have been written as a manual for the instruction of new converts.

Significantly, the gospels contain not only an account of what Jesus did, but also of what he taught. For Christians ancient or modern, it is vitally important to know what Jesus said. He taught in the synagogue and in the temple. He taught the great multitudes and the small group of his closest followers in gatherings outdoors. His parabolic method is a model of speaking to human interest and need.

In like manner, both ministries are found in Acts and the epistles. In the second chapter of Acts it can be seen that when three thousand were converted, they were immediately enrolled in a program of teaching, fellowship, and worship. Evangelism and education went hand in hand from the first day of the church's existence. Preaching and teaching were the great functions of the apostles. These activities were inextricably woven together in the accounts.

The epistles are themselves instruments of teaching by which church leaders instructed the membership in doctrine and practice. Paul, for example, gave a long series of instructions to the Corinthians in response to their questions and reports he had received. In the same document, he proclaimed his gospel of the saving power of God in Christ. The prophetic concerns for knowing about the nature and will of God as wells as having a personal relationship with God as Redeemer are reunited in the letters of Paul.

Similar examples may be drawn from other epistles. Even Revelation has a climactic word about these two ministries. There is no better example anywhere of teaching cast into a form that fits the situation of the hearers. The persecuted, beleagured members of the seven churches in Asia needed desperately to know that God's side would eventually win out in spite of all appearances. John told them this in such a vivid way that the could never forget it.

Correspondingly, the great passages of faith in the final outcome of God's plan as seen in Revelation are designed to evoke stronger faith or new faith in those who read them. To comprehend that God reigns with all power, to know that Jesus promises a crown of life to those who endure, to hear him say, "Behold, I stand at the door and knock"—all these are powerful incentives to faith and commitment. Clearly, Revelation is deeply consonant with both evangelism and education. In fact the Bible as a whole commands that both these ministries be carried out to the fullest of the strength and ability that the church can muster.

Evangelism and Education in Practice

In some periods the church has taken this mandate seriously, and these have been the eras of the church's greatest impact upon the world. One such epoch was the time from the beginnings of Christianity down to the accession of Constantine the Great. The winning of converts resulted not only from preaching, but also from personal witnessing and from the example of the martyrs, who by their brave suffering demonstrated that here was a faith worth dying for. The Catechumenate assured that all who were admitted into full fellowship had a firm grounding in Christian doctrine. The church grew apace, and it exerted a profound influence on the Roman world.

Other epochs may be cited, such as the period of the Reformation and immediately after, when great emphasis fell upon salvation by grace and on an informed laity; or the period, roughly 1740-1900, when revivalism and the rise of modern Christian education coincided to form a powerful combination.

From a practical standpoint, therefore, mutual respect and cooperation between leaders in evangelism and religious education are desirable in the highest degree. Then how does this concern our mutual faith?

Evangelism and Education in the Light of Faith

If there is to be a new era of power in which the life of the church is heightened and informed by the best of both kinds of ministry, there must be a theology which makes this possible. Such is to be found only in the sound doctrine of the Incarnation. In the past liberalism has sometimes so emphasized the humanity of Jesus as to lose sight of his divinity. Conservatism has often so emphasized the divinity of Christ as to lose sight of his humanity.

The doctrine of Incarnation makes it clear that there can be no separation. Jesus is the Christ; both his humanity and his divinity are real. Without humanity the earthly life of Jesus would be a sham; without divinity his power to save would be nil.

Not surprisingly, then, Jesus in his ministry embodies both evangelism and education. His call is one to follow him, to accept his kingdom, to believe the gospel. He tells parables to demonstrate the loving concern of God for the lost and the joy of participation in the eschatalogical feat. At the same time Jesus is the great Teacher: one who knows how to speak to the deepest concerns of his hearers, to use real-life situations as occasions for learning, to paint word pictures that make a point unforgettable, to ask questions that elicit new insights.

Jesus raised no partition between evangelism and education. His parables regularly combined elements from both faith-commitment and nurture, and he lived both of them daily. Faith in Christ requires commitment to two kinds of ministry. Christians may distinguish between them cognitively, but they may not neglect either one, nor pit one against the other. . . .

One of the places where evangelism and Christian education must be taken more seriously is in the seminaries that train pastors for local congregations. Unfortunately most of the stress there has been on systematic theology, on content courses of doctrine and biblical materials, to the detriment of the fields of practical theology. Theological and biblical studies are essential, but until ministers learn something about how to communicate such insights, they may as well be locked in a vault and the key dropped into the ocean.

When evangelism and Christian education take not only themselves, but also each other, as the most serious business at hand, there will be a continuation of what is best from the past; and there will be new, creative, fertile, effective ideas and programs under constant development. The few examples given here barely hint at the possibilities.

The key to effective ministries is to be found in dialogue—dialogue in the sense of an open, authentic exchange of thoughts and feelings. There must be dialogue, dialogue, and more dialogue, until our difference become only functional. Then they will constitute the dynamic for a quantum leap into the future.

If this spirit prevails, the future is not discouraging. It is too early to claim victory in our era, but not to express optimism. Working together in fellowship, cooperation, and love, we can leave the results in the hands of God.

A Policy Statement of the National Council of Churches in the United States of America, adopted by the Governing Board March 3, 1976.

Evangelism Today

Introductory Statement: This is a statement that was developed by the Working Group on Evangelism of the DCS, and expresses a common ground where representatives of a wide range of churches outside the National Council of Churches could meet with those who are members of the NCC. It is not intended as a comprehensive theological treatise on evangelism, but as a corrective to the recent dichotomy between "personal" evangelism and "social action." It is a description of the past and present pilgrimage, and so does not attempt to address the problems yet to be encountered.

One way of setting forth what evangelism means in the ecumenical experience today is to review the journey of the past twenty-five years of that experience—a period in which evangelism has been a central issue in American church life. During this period of changing concepts of evangelism, its fullness has never been totally disclosed at any one time or place, and this statement does not attempt a final or definitive description of it.

In the 1950s, two major methods were utilized in evangelism: mass meeting campaigns and lay visitation programs, both inviting persons to make decisions for Jesus Christ. Although other factors probably contributed, these modes of sharing the gospel coincided in the 1950s with a season of growth in church membership unparallelled in American church history.

However, growth in church membership and calling people to Christian discipleship were not necessarily the same. In the early 1960s it became apparent that for many people, joining the church had not produced a significant change of attitude or behavior. This failure of new church members to be enlisted in a pilgrimage toward fuller Christian discipleship called into question the effectiveness of the methods then being used. There followed an intense theological re-examination of what the demands of Christian discipleship should mean both for individuals and for society.

In the process of re-examination, the practice of evangelism as a congregational function in which people are confronted with the gospel and called to Christian discipleship was minimized in those denominations which were working together in the National Council of Churches.

Denominational attention was focused on social injustices, and efforts were made to mobilize members to help rectify them. A false division resulted. Instead of social awareness and action being seen as natural expressions of Christian discipleship to which people are called by evangelism, social action was thought to be a contrast and corrective to evangelism. In this mistaken polarization between them, both—and the whole life of the church—were weakened.

Today we can see the futility of that polarization, but the churches still seem strangely bound by a reluctance to name the Name of Jesus as Lord and Savior. Christians seem to lack the facility today to exclaim with excitement, "Jesus loves me; therefore, I love you." At this moment in history, there is great need for the churches to recover the ability to name the Name of Jesus Christ as Lord and Savior and to bear witness to that name in word and deed.

But naming the Name and bearing witness to it must be better understood: the commitment to Jesus Christ is a profound event. It is a *personal* event; by the power of the Holy Spirit sinners experience the divine forgiveness and commit themselves to live obediently to Christ the living Lord. It is a *social* event; relationships with friends, neighbors and family are radically altered by the revolutionary demands and allowances of divine love. It is a *community* event; it engrafts one into the community of believers, the church. It is a *public* event; new confrontations with the institutions of society occur, for the "principalities and powers" which impoverish and enslave humanity cannot go unchallenged by Christians!

Commitment to Jesus Christ must be made in the context of the issues posed for us by the moment of history in which we find ourselves—history in which God is at work, through us and sometimes in spite of us. That commitment to Jesus Christ must have an impact on the issues of social and economic justice through the stewardship, integrity and interdependence of Christian disciples. Thereby commitment to Jesus Christ is inescapably a personal social community and public historical event which affects the world and the human beings in it for whom Christ died.

Commitment to Jesus Christ is not a once-for-all event. It is the beginning of one's spiritual pilgrimage of discipleship. Those who are disciples of Christ face continual turning points which offer new experiences rooted in being "born anew to a living hope." We never move beyond the need to hear the renewing call to "repent and believe in the gospel," in order to live more obediently to the word of the Lord in every area of life, turning from the dead values of self-centered living, acquisitive consumption and upward social striving.

Commitment to Jesus Christ means to embrace more completely in our *personal* lives the new way of life which God's grace initiates, manifesting the Spirit's fruit of love, joy, peace, goodness, meekness, gentleness, and self-control. Commitment to Jesus Christ means in our *social* life to love others more deeply, even as Christ loves us and gave himself for us, a love which is giving, accepting, forgiving, seeking and helping. Commitment to Jesus Christ in *community* life means to be called out from the isolation of individualism, from conformity to the ways of the world into the fellowship of disciples which is the church, where by obedience we discover freedom, by humble service we are fulfilled, by sharing the sufferings of others we are made whole. Commitment to Jesus Christ in our *public* lives means to be engaged more earnestly in the work not only of relieving the poor and hungry but removing the causes of poverty and hunger in the struggle to remedy both inequities and iniquities, in the liberation of the oppressed and the vindication of the deprived, in the establishment of God's rule in the affairs of humanity. Commitment to Jesus Christ brings confidence that however dark the present hour, the ultimate victory is assured through him who is the Lord.

The task of evangelism today is calling people to repentance, to faith in Jesus Christ, to study God's word, to continue steadfast in prayer, and to bearing witness to Him. This is a primary function of the church in its congregational, denominational and ecumenical manifestations. It challenges the most creative capabilities in the churches while at the same time depending upon the Holy Spirit to be the real evangelist.

Now, after the journey of the past twenty-five years, we can call upon people to confess the Name of Jesus Christ and to bear witness to that Name in their lives with a fuller understanding of Christian discipleship and a deeper commitment to share the good news we have found.